ADVANCE ACCLAIM
for
"IT RUNS IN MY FAMILY"
Overcoming the Legacy of Family Illness

"This empowering book demonstrates that the 'family' illness doesn't have to be passed from generation to generation. Step by step, it will help you uncover your own uniqueness and free you from reliving old scripts, detrimental to your health and well-being. Let it be your guide to healing yourself and your family."

—DR. BERNIE SIEGEL
Author of the bestseller, Love, Medicine & Miracles

"'It Runs in My Family' is must reading for anyone who cares about staying alive. With a most practical and lively style, Barth makes incredibly clear the fundamental connections between our lives, our health, and our families and provides a roadmap for empowering ourselves to live healthy lives."

—MONICA MCGOLDRICK, ACSW, PH.D.
Director,
The Family Institute of New Jersey

"Barth's presentation of the ways that individuals can wrest control of their health away from the grip of family myths embodies the optimism and energy she prescribes. 'You can do it,' she says. After reading her book, you will believe you can."

—LEE COMBRINCK-GRAHAM, M.D.
Child and Family Psychiatrist

"Insightful and empowering! Laced with poignant stories, important facts, and crisp, clear guidelines, 'It Runs in My Family' provides a map for discovering a path to a healthy lifestyle. Using a family systems perspective, Barth shows how to detour around negative family legacies, creating new inroads to health and healing."

—CONSTANCE R. AHRONS, PH.D.
Professor of Sociology,
Associate Director,
Marriage and Family
Therapy Programs,
University of Southern California;
Author of The Good Divorce;
Coauthor of Divorced Families

"Passivity in the face of family relationships, family scripts, and family illness can be deadly. Dr. Barth's book provides us with a structure and a pathway to do battle."

—PHILIP J. GUERIN, JR., M.D.
Director,
Center for Family Learning,
Rye Brook, NY

"IT RUNS
IN MY FAMILY"

Overcoming the Legacy
of Family Illness

Joan C. Barth

BRUNNER/MAZEL Publishers • NEW YORK

Library of Congress Cataloging-in-Publication Data

Barth, Joan, C.
  "It runs in my family" : overcoming the legacy of family illness /
Joan C. Barth.
      p.   cm.
  Includes bibliographical references and index.
  ISBN 0-87630-712-8
  1. Medicine, Popular.   2. Medicine, Preventive.   3. Self-care,
Health.   4. Medical genetics.   5. Genealogy.   I. Title.
  [DNLM: 1. Family Health.   2. Attitude to Health.   3. Family
Therapy.   WM 430.5.F2 B284i 1993]
RC82.B39   1993
616.'042—dc20
DNLM/DLC
for Library of Congress   93-24660
                                                                  CIP

Published by
BRUNNER/MAZEL, INC.
19 Union Square West
New York, New York 10003

Manufactured in the United States of America

10   9   8   7   6   5   4   3   2   1

To my mother
Henrietta Moran
who taught me never to give up

Contents

Acknowledgments

Like the gestation period of a baby, this book has been a long time being born. There are many people who have served as midwives to the birth.

First and foremost among them is my daughter, Trish. She "nudged" me to get the work done and kept me on track. She knew just the right time to send a funny card or a bouquet of flowers.

Others who helped me are numerous. Their help has been major or minor, but without them I could not have succeeded. Let me list them in no special order: Gladys Valcourt, Florence Kaslow, Pat Reardon, Marilee Goldberg, Gunter David, Sandy Coleman, Charlie Gerras, Jill Derstine, Laxmikant, Marie Bradley, Tom Ford, Fred Hilmer, Christine Colgan, Martha Ann Rayne, Louise Lee Roche, Peggy O'Neill, George and Karen White, Valerie and Jay Smith, Lou and Libby White, Nick and Marjory Morgan, Pat Martindell, Bob Meehan, Kay Alderfer, Cheryl Michael, Hannelore Hahn and the IWWG., and my editor, Natalie Gilman.

Thanks also go to those nearly 500 people who were willing to answer my health questionnaire.

My clients have shared their lives with me for the last 19 years. Their openness has helped me grow and I hope has made me a better therapist for them. I thank them all, particularly the ones who shared the legacy of physical illness in their families. While the case studies in this book have been compiled from real people, names and locations have been changed to protect privacy.

Finally, besides my daughter, Trish, I want to thank the rest of my family for their love and support: Bob, my husband; Stephen, Kathy, and Mackenzie Barth; and Rich Tatar.

My parents, Mike and Henrietta Colgan, raised me to believe in myself. I am sorry they and my sisters, Evelyn and Christine, and my brother, Richie, are no longer alive to enjoy the book publication.

Without the help of all these people, I could not have finished the book. I am blessed by each of them.

Introduction

All myths are magical. Classic myths often include a beautiful princess who is powerless and a handsome prince who will save her, despite enormous odds.

The legacy of family illness is like that. The members of the family—including the beautiful princess—lie powerless in the face of family illness. Nothing they do can spare them from the inevitable.

Only the handsome prince—be it the magic of God or of medicine—can overcome the threat they face. Sick people await deliverance from forces outside themselves—often in vain. People not yet sick do the same.

They wait for magic.

The legacy of family illness sometimes convinces them that nothing they do can overcome the inevitability of getting the illness and dying from it at a time preordained by family "history," no matter how early in life. They are doomed.

"IT RUNS IN MY FAMILY" is not another form of passive magic. Rather it is a blueprint for actively designing good health and long life.

Taking charge of living a healthy lifestyle is very powerful. Instead of believing we are doomed to follow in the footsteps of our forebears, we can empower ourselves to blaze our own paths.

We can give up smoking, eat a better diet, begin an exercise program, avoid undue stress. In other words, we can add techniques to our lives and develop new habits that improve our health.

When I was growing up, my brother, sisters, and I had a saying, "I learned it at my mother's knee." We said it when something we did was a long-standing habit that we did automatically. We all learn certain health behaviors as young children.

Many behaviors learned in the family affect our health.

Overcoming the legacy of expecting poor health is harder to do than to receive positive expectations in the first place. However, such change is possible. This book provides specific methods of creating change. It outlines what can be done to make your future healthy. Behaviors, beliefs, and support systems that positively expect health are available. How to develop them and then how to use them effectively will be described.

In order to take charge of your future, you must recognize that you have the power to do so. Feeling helpless and hopeless does not lead to your empowering yourself about your health.

What do you envision for yourself? Is it a life of zest and liveliness or one of expectation of doom? As an adult, you can expect to add more maxims about health to the ones you heard as a child: "You have to expect that after 35 . . ." or "You're not as young as you used to be."

These are as tempting to believe as the original dicta you heard as a youngster. Do not let them design your future. You deserve a life of good health. You have the power to accomplish that.

This book will provide you with methods of voluntarily disinheriting yourself of health legacies you do not want.

Chapter 1, Family Legacies, describes the things we inherit from our families.

Chapter 2, Your Family Tree: The Art of Drawing Genograms, explains how we can draw an annotated family tree to help design our futures.

Chapter 3, Life Drawing: Picturing Yourself and Your Legacy, describes how to develop a Life Drawing in order to see, graphically, the patterns of family illness.

Chapter 4, Fatalists: "It's No Use," describes those who see themselves as powerless in the face of family illness are described.

In Chapter 5, Fighters: "I Make My Own Future," those who refuse the family legacy of illness are described.

Chapter 6, Fatalist or Fighter: Which Will You Be? helps you determine how you will live your life.

Chapter 7, You and the Health Care Practitioner, gives suggestions on how to get the help you need.

Chapter 8 on Beating the Odds tells you explicitly how to refuse the legacy of illness and early death, and assure yourself good health.

Finally, Chapter 9, Implications for Therapists, outlines methods therapists can use to help clients deal with family illnesses.

Activities suggested at the end of each chapter will help provide you with options for good health. You may want to keep a notebook of your responses to the activities.

This book makes a distinction between what you can change and what you can't. It is a book of hope.

Hope is given to those who come from families in which there is a history of cancer, heart disease, Huntingdon's Chorea, diabetes, and other illnesses that seem relentless in their generational recurrence.

In my own family, there have been many cases of cancer and of heart disease. I do not want my children or grandchildren to feel they are at the mercy of history. Neither do I want my clients and friends, whose families have a history of illness, to feel doomed.

Let me help you empower yourself to a life of health and zest.

1

FAMILY LEGACIES

Miguel Hernandez shifted his 83-year-old body in a chair at his daughter's dining room table. His fingers smoothed the creases in the lace tablecloth in rhythm with his words as he reminisced about his grandmother, Constancia. She had endowed him with a legacy of good health. "My grandmother was a little mite of a thing—weighed maybe a hundred pounds. She lived to be 115."

Miguel waved his gnarled, sturdy hand about a foot above the tabletop to indicate his grandmother's size.

"But every day she worked hard on the farm. She milked the cows, fed the chickens, planted the garden. She was full of pep.

"Ate lots of her own vegetables and, once in a while, killed a chicken to make *asopao*—chicken and rice.

"She and her oldest son, my uncle Tomas, loved to play dominoes. They were ruthless. Nobody could beat them.

"I played pinochle with her every Friday night until she was 113. She liked to win and," Miguel lowered his voice as if Constancia still might hear him, "would cheat a little if she was losing. She was a real card.

"After working all day Constancia would take a walk down the hill and look at her land. She'd walk back up to the house and pull a rocker out to the front of the verandah.

"From that spot she could see the whole farm laid out in front

1

of her—her vegetable garden, her flowers, her chickens, the couple of milk cows. Constancia would sigh with contentment at the sight of it all.

"She had real oompah."

The legacy of hard work and small indulgences Miguel inherited gives him an active vision of his future. He does not foresee a life of feeble health nor a mind vacuous and meandering. Rather, he imagines himself as interesting and lively. "I expect to live to be at least 100."

Miguel has received a legacy of healthy, long-lived relatives. He has always seen them hard at work, joyous, eating sensibly, surrounded by loved ones. He expects to follow in their footsteps.

The father of one of my friends, Miguel retired from his career in neurochemistry nearly 20 years ago. Now, in his 80s, he continues to go to the races, root for a baseball team on which his nephew plays professional ball, and visit his adult children several thousand miles away. His only curtsy to age is having "Meals on Wheels" delivered to his home each day.

At family weddings, Miguel is always the center of much attention. He dances with the most beautiful women and revels in their telling him how charming and delightful he is. They laugh at his stories and engage him in stimulating conversation. Wherever he is, there is zest and good humor. The legacy of good health and liveliness he received from his grandmother is always apparent.

AN ATTITUDE OF DOOM

A very different legacy was inherited by Becky Shore.

Becky entered my office a few months ago, for the first time. She folded her lanky body into a rocking chair and began to spin out her story.

On the recommendation of her career counselor, Becky, a 36-year-old advertising account executive, had begun therapy to strengthen her presentation of herself.

Becky had been interviewed for seven jobs. While having

excellent experience and education for each of the jobs, Becky failed to land any of them.

Her career counselor believed Becky had an attitude that prevented her from appearing self-confident. Hiring her meant that personnel directors had to have more belief in Becky than she had in herself.

After we drew up the Shore family tree (her genogram), Becky told me of her future goals. She wanted 1) to be married, 2) to have children, and 3) to run her own advertising business.

Only men in the family had run their own businesses. Women in the Shore family had attained the first two of Becky's goals, being married and having children.

Many women relatives of Becky also had had hysterectomies.

"I have a box in the corner of my bedroom. I put all the projects I don't have time for in there. When I have my hysterectomy, I have six weeks worth of reading, needlepoint, rug-making supplies, photos to mount in scrapbooks in the box.

"I'll have lots to keep me busy during my recovery."

Becky had experienced no symptoms of needing a hysterectomy. Her periods were regular. There was no spotting between periods.

She didn't consider that a change in her attitude of inevitability might have some power to help keep her well.

In other ways, Becky was a Fatalist also, a victim of outside forces.

She had lived with a man, Len, for the past three years. They had no definite plans for marriage.

"We'll see what happens."

The first of Becky's goals—being married—did not seem likely in the foreseeable future.

Besides Len, Becky also doted on her nieces and nephew, the children of her twin brother and his wife. The children called her "Auntie B" and were very happy whenever she arrived.

As much as she enjoyed them, she always waited for a phone call from her brother with an invitation to visit. She never simply dropped in or telephoned to ask if it was a good time to go to the house.

The children, who might have substituted for those she did

not have, as yet, were part of her life only when she was invited into their lives by someone else.

Becky did not have a savings fund set up for the start of her own business. Nor did she keep a list of possible clients.

All her future goals seemed to be daydreams. Becky believed that what was meant to happen would happen.

LEGACIES

Becky's ancesters might have left her the following will:

"To my beloved son, Andrew, I leave my high blood pressure.

"For the many times she soothed me when I was concerned about financial problems, I leave my daughter, Rose, my diabetes.

"To my other daughter, Becky, who welcomed me into her house to live in my old age, I leave my hysterectomy."

Miguel's story shows a very different kind of legacy. The following will might have been written by his ancestors.

"For the many delicious meals she made me, I leave Angie my fine china.

"For the times he fixed my car when the mechanics gave up all hope of its resurrection, I leave Tom 10 percent of my monies.

"Maria was always cheerful when I awakened her at 2 A.M. because I was worried about noises I heard in my garage. I leave her all my antiques—furniture and knickknacks."

No one consciously plans to bequeath his or her ills to a loved one. Yet, unconsciously, that is what many family members expect to inherit. They are not surprised to develop high blood pressure, cancer, or diabetes, for example.

Yet legacies can be good or bad.

WHICH LEGACY TO ACCEPT?

You can legally refuse to accept a legacy. Few people so empower themselves. They may believe that what someone gave them they must accept.

Look around you. In the room you're sitting in, are there any items you received as gifts but don't particularly want? Do you fail to discard them, for whatever reason? Do you feel helpless to throw them out?

That may indicate how destined you feel to accept family legacies. If you feel powerless about an insignificant gift, how powerful do you feel about those that affect your life deeply?

After all, an ugly vase is one thing. A legacy of heart disease is quite another.

Do you feel powerless to create your own lifestyle? Must you follow a forebear whose life was filled with illness and ended in an early (before age 55) death?

WHICH MODEL TO FOLLOW?

Like Miguel, we all choose which lifestyle to follow. It may be that of a Constancia with her oompah, her love of cards and hard work, and her sociability. It may be an Uncle Harry who was very funny, overweight, a pool hall wizard, and a heavy drinker. He died at 45. What about an Aunt Ethel who played the organ at church every Sunday, learned to pilot an airplane at 87, dug her own vegetable garden into her 90s, participated in the senior citizens' marathon every year, and died in her sleep at 101? Maybe it is someone like my mother, who rode her horse through six feet of snow to school, clobbered a snake with a 2x4, and read the racing results while she ironed. It may be Ashley Montague, who in his 80s can give an erudite talk, without notes, for two hours. Or a friend who fulfilled a lifelong dream and bought a farm and two horses in her 50s.

The models of health you choose to imitate are usually relatives or other persons you are deeply touched by in one way or another. You think, "I hope I am just like her when I'm old," or "I'll probably get cancer like he did."

You are unlikely to choose an ordinary model. You are drawn to the thought of being *very healthy* into old age or dying at an *early age*, just as your model did.

WHY NOW?

Did your chosen health model develop illness at the same stage in life at which you are?

I believe that many illnesses are dormant. When they surface, it is because of the present need for what they do. That may have been true of the emulated ancestor, as well. He or she may have needed the family illness when thwarted by the same life issues you are.

Why does the illness occur now? It may protect you from some job dilemma or excuse you from events you wish to avoid.

A family illness has the immediate effect of mobilizing the family to respond as it always has to that event.

"We Shore women always have hysterectomies."

"Only God can help."

"I'm sending Mary flowers and flying up there this weekend."

"Don't give in to it. Fight."

Being resigned, praying a lot, spending more time with the sick person may be customary ways the family responds to illness.

One cancer patient told me the best thing about her illness was that her brother visited her after having no contact for 20 years.

The answer to the question "Why now?" may require additional help.

A health journal sometimes provides that help, graphically.

HEALTH JOURNAL

A health journal is a record of physiological events, like a cold, a stiff neck, a wart—minor things we fail to recall, as well as major events, such as a heart attack, gall bladder surgery. Life events—loss of a job, turning 40, birth of first grandchild—are also included.

Following is a portion of a health journal:

April 20, 1993

First robin of Spring.
Pain in right shoulder.
Have been typing into my computer
    to get the paper finished.
Received IRS refund check. Very Happy.
Left leg very sore.

Sometimes events that appear to have no connection, do. Once, when I went over my health journal for the previous five years, I discovered that the only time I was absent from work due to illness was during the month of February.

The following winter, I planned happy events in February.

My husband and I took a short holiday to the Caribbean. I bought tickets to the Philadelphia Flower Show. I kept the tickets, which were printed on bright yellow paper, in my appointment book where I saw them every day.

Winters in Pennsylvania can be long and dreary. Having some goal that reminds me that Spring will ultimately arrive helps both my mental and physical health.

PSYCHOMATIC

All illness is psychosomatic. Mind and body, psyche and soma. What affects one affects the other. Neither is an entity unto itself. Like Siamese twins, one is connected to the other.

Becky's belief that she is helpless to change the family legacy has an effect on her body. Her mind is powerful enough to make her body helpless to be well.

The same is true of Miguel. He believes that no matter what he does he has inherited a legacy of long life and good health. His mind has an effect on his body.

The body also has an effect on the mind. When people are sick, say with pneumonia, they cannot concentrate on reading. When the body is out of balance, the mind responds as well.

Saying people have a "psychosomatic" illness is a way some

people have of denigrating the health problems of others. I believe that rather than minimizing illness by saying it is "psychosomatic," you should accept that all illnesses involve the mind as well as the body. You cannot divide yourself into parts.

When my husband had a heart attack, 16 years ago, some of his cardiologists dealt with him as if he had only a heart. They did not examine other parts of his body. However, one of the cardiologists insisted Bob send letters of resignation to all the organizations in his appointment book which did not give him pleasure. This doctor saw that people are made up of mind and body. They have power to influence both of them.

DO WE INHERIT OUR ILLNESSES?

Of the three major causes of death in the U.S., all are considered failures of the body : 1) cardiovascular diseases, 2) cancer, and 3) cerebrovascular diseases.

The National Cancer Institute forecasts that if their recommendations are adopted—to refrain from smoking, to make changes in diet, to have frequent tests for cancer, and to use current treatment methods, 25 percent to 50 percent of people who now die of cancer will live to an older age.

But to do that you have to believe you are the master of your fate. You must believe you can change your behaviors and that such change will have a positive influence on your health.

If one of your grandparents or parents suffered from heart disease, hypertension, or cancer, you probably believe chances are better than normal that you will too. Seventy-four percent of the nearly 500 respondents to a survey I conducted on health reported their belief that "illnesses run in my family."

Yet medical science fails to support such a high incidence of inherited illness. In other words, there is no biological reason for the fears of most people about family illness. Is there an inheritance nonetheless? What is inherited?

You inherit lifestyles. You were taught them in your family.

That was true of tuberculosis, for example, one of the three major causes of death in 1900.

Tuberculosis was viewed as a family illness because members of the same family developed and often died from it.

Instead, eventually, it was learned that the reason family members shared the illness was that they all drank from the same impure source of water, drank unpasteurized milk, lived in unclean conditions.

Once those situations were resolved, and even before effective antibiotics became available in the 40s, tuberculosis was on the way to being eradicated.

People, themselves, changed their behavior through new learning. Credit for major change has been given to elementary school children.

Posters about cleanliness in elementary schools were responsible for educating children about their power to be well.

State laws required food handlers to wash their hands after using toilets. Hospitals required staff to wash their hands before touching patients.

Through the efforts of health workers and other individuals, rather than by means of miracle drugs, tuberculosis was basically eradicated during that period.

Those people changed their lifestyles. So can you.

LEARNING

As adults, we must often unlearn bad lessons we learned as children. Babies learn internally, from their inner messages. They cry when they feel hungry, wet, or in pain. After a number of months, they learn that if they act a certain way, adults who care for them will respond in certain ways. When no one responds to them, babies stop crying. They become quiet and morose. Their health is affected.

External pressures become noticeable to babies, sometime in the first year of life. They learn that playing "so big" results in adults laughing. They learn that if they kiss someone, they are cooed at.

They also learn that if they are not as peppy as usual or do not eat all their dinner, their parents place their hands on the baby's forehead and ask if they are okay. In spite of the fact that babies cannot articulate their ideas, they learn about the feelings of the people around them. Habits that are related to health are learned very early.

Since health habits and attitudes are learned, they can be unlearned.

Some families teach habits of poor health. Those families teach that eating "junk" foods is all right, that living under high levels of chronic stress is necessary for success, that being on a new diet several times a year is commonplace. They do not teach that high levels of stress are to be considered rare occurrences, that what one eats makes a difference to one's health, that a level of exercise is necessary, that maintaining strong friendships is important.

A child learns what he or she was taught. Watch a three year old approach a hot light on a Christmas tree. "No," says the approaching child. The parent no longer has to warn the child. The child does his or her own warning.

Later in life, the admonitions remain. Adults rarely say them aloud. Rather they remain as a part of their "inner dialogue," the voices we all have that urge us to do or to avoid certain things.

Miguel Hernandez, whom you met at the beginning of this chapter, learned from his grandmother that good health can be expected. She also taught him good health habits. "I'll live to a ripe old age. We Hernandez' live to be at least a hundred."

There are two methods of learning—from the outside or from inside. Some people like to have an external authority lay out the chances they have of attaining good health. But other people like to sift information through their own filters. Unless something rings true to them, they place little faith in it. It doesn't matter, for example, that a renowned specialist tells them they have three months to live, they believe they will get well. On the other hand, external learners are plummeted into a deep depression upon hearing such a sentence.

Internal or external learning techniques influence people to maintain wellness, to regain good health after an illness or to resign themselves to death. The legacies you receive as a child often predict what you believe as an adult. However, if you did not learn positive attitudes about health as a child, you can reprogram yourself as an adult.

EXPECTATIONS

From your learning as a child, you expect certain things to happen when you grow up. You may not expand those learnings in adulthood and, as a result, much of what you know may be out-of-sync with your age. It is as if you continue to use training wheels after you have learned to ride a bike.

As a child, you may have been taught to do something a certain way. You may not alter it as an adult. Are you still doing things automatically rather than deciding if you want to do it that way?

Expectations you keep from childhood may not enhance your life as a grown person. You may expect others to guess what you are feeling: "If he loved me, he would have known how I felt." Parents are the only ones who intuitively know what each cry or silence of their children means. However, you can spend the rest of your life expecting to find someone who knows you intimately with no verbal assistance from you.

And you may expect your body to run on automatic, too. After all, your mother didn't exercise at a gym. But she may have ironed, washed windows, walked to the store each day and carried the groceries home. Your father may have taken public transportation to work after walking 10 blocks to the bus, climbed steps on the job, brought a lunch from home made of healthy foods, shovelled snow, mowed the yard. In other words, your parents may have exercised as a part of their daily lives.

Their expectations were based on the kind of lifestyles they had learned. But you may be a pioneer. Life for you isn't the way it was for your parents or grandparents. You can decide to leave your children a legacy of expectations based on a new lifestyle. Your children do not need to receive fatalistic attitudes from you.

FATALISTS

Fatalists believe they are victims. They have a "what will be, will be" attitude. They do not believe their actions influence their future.

One of my clients, a woman with diabetes, provides a good example of a Fatalist. As they left the diabetes clinic after her annual checkup, Lonnie Rourke asked her daughter to have a hot-fudge sundae with her. Lonnie had just been warned of the worsening state of her health. She believes that she can do nothing to make any difference about her diabetes. Changing her diet won't help. "After all," she says, "didn't many of my relatives die of diabetes?"

She is a Fatalist, one of those people who believe that they are destined to develop poor health and die young, regardless of what they do.

SKEPTICS

Skeptics are a subgroup of Fatalists who work hard at being healthy. They exercise, eat sensibly, maintain a healthy level of stress, don't smoke. Yet they worry that their efforts are in vain. They are apprehensive that their best efforts cannot overcome a family history of disease.

A participant at one of my workshops on family health legacies, Beth James is a 32-year-old financial analyst and a Skeptic. She works out at least five times a week, stays slim, doesn't smoke, meditates, practices stress management. Yet, she believes that all her efforts will not keep her from developing high blood pressure or heart disease since those two diseases show up frequently in her family history.

In my view, Beth is likely to develop one of those illnesses because she believes her efforts are fated to result in failure. If she programs herself to expect to live a long life and continues her healthy lifestyle, I doubt if worry alone will kill her early, but it is not helpful.

A healthy way of life without the belief that it is powerful is not enough to attain and maintain good health. Belief *alone* is not enough; behavior patterns *alone* are not enough. *Both are necessary.*

FIGHTERS

Fighters believe they will benefit from working towards being healthy. Regardless of their family health histories, they are certain that eating well and moderately, exercising, not smoking, and keeping stress within limits will increase their likelihood of being fit.

David Fretz comes from a family where many males have had heart disease. All of them led sedentary lives.

David climbs mountains every chance he gets. When he feels his heart pumping vigorously on the slopes, he doesn't worry that he will have a heart attack. Instead, he congratulates his body for doing what it is supposed to do.

Fighters refuse the family legacy. They are unwilling to accept the threat of a life overshadowed by fate. Instead they live a lifestyle devoted to health. When faced with physical maladies, they trust in their ability to overcome them. They may not expect to return fully to their former perfect health after experiencing a disease, but they do expect to live a fruitful life.

ACTIVITIES

1. What are the legacies you inherited from your family of origin? What ones do you treasure?
2. What legacies will you leave your children, brothers, and sisters?

2

YOUR FAMILY TREE
The Art of Drawing Genograms

The fresh dabs of paint on her skirt were all in primary colors—yellow, blue and red.

Maude Carter stood back and looked at the family tree with satisfaction. She had been painting it for days. She could imagine it hanging above her father's office fireplace. She always asked herself before his birthday, "What can I give a man who has everything?"

Darnell Carter IV was a successful lawyer who was celebrating his 50th birthday next week, the first Darnell Carter in four generations to reach that age. The family tree showed that her father's father, Darnell III, was born on March 5, 1914 and died June 12, 1963. Her great-grandfather, Darnell II, was born April 16, 1886 and died May 8, 1934. The first Darnell was born June 23, 1861 and died October 18, 1908.

How different from his daughter's painting was the genogram, or family tree, Darnell IV had developed in my office.

Darnell IV had visited me because of the aftermath of a gunshot wound. He had received physical therapy and regained most of his former flexibility, but wanted to know why he had lost most of his exuberance for life.

In order to put the event into the context of Darnell IV's life, I asked him to draw a genogram.

A genogram is a family tree with juice. It isn't a sterile

account of births and deaths. Rather, it notes not only births and deaths, but also the circumstances around them. It also notes other significant events in a family's life—a man who went to war at 18, a woman diagnosed "hysterical" and hospitalized for two years, a man who won a Pulitzer Prize for journalism.

Darnell's genogram also showed that the men in his family had died before the age of 50 for the last four generations. It also noted that each of them died from heart disease.

Darnell wanted to leave a more hopeful legacy to his son, Darnell V. In order to do that, he lived a different lifestyle from his forebears. Unlike their "portly" figures, Darnell IV's figure was slim through means of regular exercise and being moderate in food and drink. "My father revelled in his glass of port before dinner. He also revelled in his whiskey before breakfast and his martinis after the glass of port in the evening."

Darnell IV had inherited the family legal business, but refused to work on weekends. Instead, he enjoyed taking his family boating on the Chesapeake and being "physical"as he taught his son and daughters to sail. He was determined the family legacy of early death for the men would end with him. (In our work, Darnell IV regained his zest for life after grieving for his lost feeling of omnipotence after being wounded in a holdup.)

A person who discovers a family history of relatives who died early of heart disease can choose to take the risk of being a smoker. He or she can choose certain things that make early death more probable.

Darnell did not feel fatalistic about his life. Instead he was determined to fight to keep himself healthy.

CHOICES

It is rare that all members of a family are Fatalists or that all are Fighters. Some may be Fatalists and others Fighters. The same event may have a certain impact on one person and a different one on his brothers or sisters. Hearing your parents say, "He had a short life but a happy one" may encourage your brother to be a heavy smoker but may encourage your sister to run two miles each day.

Many things are learned from the sayings our families make about health. "Eat, drink, and be merry for tomorrow we die," or "You'll never make it past 30," or "You're like all the other Morton men, they have heart attacks before they're 40," or "When your number's up, it's up." All those statements may have a serious effect on health. They mold your thinking about how sick or healthy you will be as an adult. And whether or not you will recover from illnesses if you get them.

Family members are not stupid. They are programmed to learn in certain ways. And they can un-program themselves. Drawing a genogram is a good way to find out what patterns have been learned.

In their book on genetics, Harsanyi and Hutton say there is no such thing as a risk-free life. However, they note, "We can make decisions about the kinds of risks we are willing to face."

FAMILY TREES

Drawing a genogram will help you make those decisions. As noted above, genograms are drawings of a family tree that include specific family events in addition to the usual dates of birth and death. The family events they include are causes of death, absences from the family (hospitalization or military service, for example), labels (the blacksheep, the smart one), who continues to live with parents into adulthood, substitute parents, governesses, difficulty at birth.

Like a program at a play, genograms tell you who is in the cast and who is important behind the scenes. The genogram provides you with a graphic representation of who the members of your family are.

Later in the chapter, we will return to the use of the genogram to discover how family members gave and got attention. For now, you can simply draw a basic genogram.

All you need is a blank sheet of paper and a pencil. (When I read, I want to read, not stop to draw. However, the drawing will ultimately prove beneficial to your health. It will take less than 15 minutes to sketch.)

DRAWING A GENOGRAM

To draw your own genogram begin with your parents, using a large square to represent your father, a circle for your mother (in Sociology, men are represented by squares, women by circles) . Add their names, birth and death dates, and anything significant about their births and causes of death (Figure 1).

Add your parents' brothers and sisters—your aunts and uncles—as they range in age from the oldest, on the far left, to the youngest, on the far right. Again, squares represent males, circles females. Make the forms fairly large as they must contain information listed later in the chapter (Figure 2). Be sure to add their names, dates of birth and deaths and any pertinent information surrounding them.

After drawing your parents' generation, place your grandparents on the level above them (Figure 3). You may have to get more information from the family recordkeeper about their generation. That may take time. For the present, put in what you know. You can add other relatives as you learn more about your family.

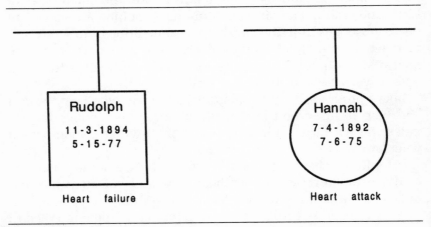

Figure 1. Your Parents

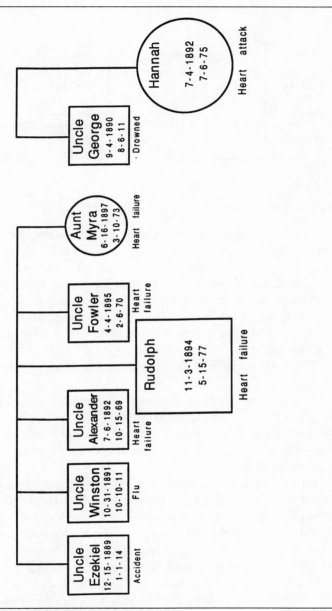

Figure 2. Your Parents and Their Siblings

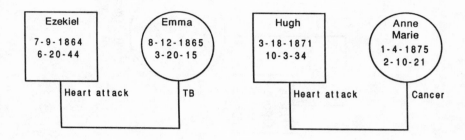

Figure 3. Your Grandparents

The final addition to your genogram is the level of you and your brothers and sisters (Figure 4). To do this, draw a line below the one for your parents. Start with your oldest sibling on the far left and move to the right as others were born. Include your full brothers and sisters (those siblings who shared the same genes you have), not stepbrothers and stepsisters or adopted siblings. Twins are indicated by a line with two lines emanating from it, as with George and Howard.

That's all that's to it. You now have a genogram of your family (Figure 5).

Review the forms to discover if you have included relatives' full names, including nicknames, dates of birth and death, illnesses, long hospitalizations, and other significant or interesting bits of information—e.g., called the "barracuda lady" and causes of death.

Do not be discouraged by gaps in information. You can fill them in as you ask more questions of family members. Creating a family genogram is a life process, not a one-time event.

You will probably discover that the history of one side of your family is more easily obtained than the other side. It can be fun and challenging to sleuth your own family history.

It may be useful to add a family chronology to your genogram. The family chronology lists significant family events in order of time: 1943–1945, Father in military service; 1943–1945, lived

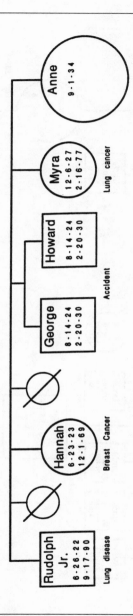

Figure 4. You and Your Siblings

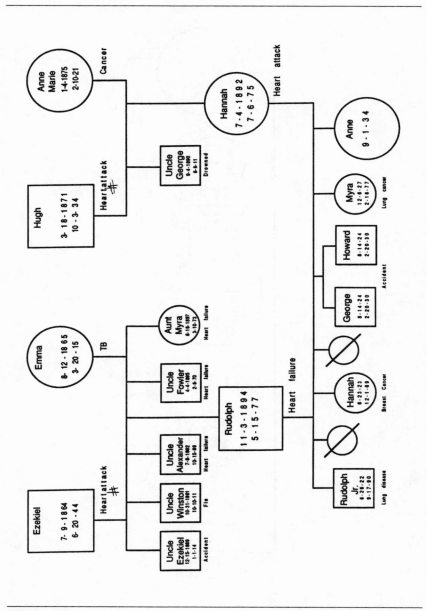

Figure 5. Your Family

with grandparents; October, 1945, Father returned; November, 1945, Grandfather died; January, 1946, moved to own house and Grandmother joined us; September, 1948, began school.

When a couple develop genograms in concert with each other, they may find that it opens discussion of important events that each had been unaware of. Learning that one's husband suffered the loss of his grandfather at the same time as his father returned from military service may allow the couple to discuss the impact of such loss on the young child.

"REWARDS" OF ILL HEALTH

For purposes of this book, focus on the physical health of family members. You may have come from a family in which there were many illnesses or one in which there were few, if any. Sadly enough, many of us are programmed to get rewarded for being sick. The behaviors rewarded at home rarely include taking life easy; rather, being sick, working hard, or being noticed in the community is what brings attention.

Poor health frequently produces attention. A client who undergoes regular dialysis says his mother will do anything for him since he has become ill. When he was well, he received little attention from her.

Children who tell their parents they don't feel like going to school that day are usually given a pat on the head and told to run along and "be a big girl or boy." Should the same child have a fever or be vomiting, he or she is kept home and given lots of attention.

The feverish child is considered "really sick," whereas the child wanting to stay at home is accused of "being a baby." Children thus learn that being physically sick is more likely to produce empathy than the expression of need does. Looking feverish is usually more apt to result in being held than does saying, "I need a hug."

When those children grow up and marry, they find that unless their spouses come from families having the same values about health, they are frustrated by what they consider to be insensitivity to their maladies.

A husband whose family urged him to stay at home when he suffered fever or headache may marry a woman whose family did not consider headache or fever as reason to forego responsibilities. When his wife encourages him to go to work when he feels ill, he may see her actions as callous. Arguments often develop between such couples.

A housewife caring for preschoolers at home may find that only when she is seriously ill does she receive sympathy and assistance from her husband. At other times, she is expected to take care of her children without help.

In fact, her husband may declare: "She has it easy. She doesn't have to contend with traffic, an unreasonable boss, deadlines. She can take a nap whenever she wants."

Only when she is physically sick does she receive acknowledgment of the important and time-consuming job she is doing.

GETTING AND GIVING ATTENTION

William James wrote: "If no one turned around as we entered, answered when we spoke or minded what we did, but if every person we met 'cut us dead,' and acted as if we were nonexisting, a kind of rage and impotent despair would spring up in us, from which the cruellest of bodily tortures would be a relief; for these would make us feel that, however bad might be our plight, we had not sunk to such a depth as to be unworthy of attention at all" (Cannon, 1942, p.173).

Children who receive attention for being sick may be fortunate to learn there are other behaviors that receive attention— making the soccer team, getting a good mark on a history exam, planting a bush in the yard. When children learn that only one behavior gets attention, they grow up without any other behavioral options.

Your mother may either notice your new outfit or the five pounds you've put on recently. She may tell you, "My, you've gotten fleshy." She may notice your physical appearance, but not give attention to your emotional needs.

Your parents may tell you that you're a great cook. Or as my father told me in the last year of his life, "We will never run out of things to talk about." Or perhaps they wait for you to telephone them, or telephone you only when they have a problem.

To determine what options prevailed in your family, please take out your Genogram again. It's time to add information to it that tells how your family members gave and got attention.

Attention-Getting and Giving Information

To the basic genogram you may now add a series of numbers from 1 to 4 that will indicate which members of the family gave and got attention for four areas of behavior: 1) illness, 2) achievement in the community, 3) work, and 4) wellness.

Attention for Illness

Most of us expect to receive attention when we are sick. It is not surprising to get flowers, candy, and cards when we have gall bladder or other surgery.

"When I got sick, for the first time in 10 years I didn't have to make supper."

"I had accumulated 207 sick days when I had a heart attack. I used most of them getting better."

Each of these speakers received attention or reward for being sick, what some experts call the "secondary gains" of illness. These gains are not consciously sought, but naturally follow being sick.

In some families, much attention is given for work, whether much work or none at all. Sayings like, "She works from dawn to dusk" or "He never did an honest day's work in his life" bring attention to the worker or the sluggard.

In particular, much attention is given to the workaholic. Granted the family may object to how seldom they see the person, but much attention is focused on him or her. (Attention means focusing on. Do not make a distinction between negative and positive attention.) Workaholics receive praise at work and criticism at home. It makes it difficult for them to know what to do. At one place, working a lot gets rewarded, at the other, it gets castigated. At both places, it gets attention.

The teenager who lies in his room listening to loud music frequently gets attention for "doing nothing." He is urged, and sometimes browbeaten, by his parents to "make yourself useful." Strategies to get him "moving" are planned.

Mark, a 16-year-old, entered family therapy because his mother was afraid he was "on drugs." Mark, a bright young man, went to his room each afternoon to listen to records. He placed his earphones on his head and turned his stereo up. At dinnertime, one of his parents physically touched him to rouse Mark from his lethargy and signal him to go to the dinner table. It was the only time he was touched by them.

It is easy to analyze what the payoff was in Mark's behavior. Not working got him some attention. It was a secondary gain.

His grandmother got attention for work, too. She was 84 years old, lived alone, and had a job taking care of "an old lady," a woman six years Margaret's junior. Margaret kept a spotless house, made her own preserves from fruits and vegetables she raised. She usually won a prize in the flower show. Trying to reach her by phone was very difficult because she was seldom home. The secondary gain she got for work was part of the family pattern.

On your genogram, begin with those who got attention for being ill. Place a 1 inside a square within the forms representing relatives who got attention whenever they were sick. Be sure to include yourself, if you've ever gotten attention for being ill.

Some of these people may have been healthy all their lives and then had a heart attack. Regardless of whether they were sick only once or were chronically sick, place a 1 inside a square within the form representing them (Figure 6.)

Attention for Community Notice

When you have completed the 1s, start with the 2s for family members who got attention for community notice. That notice could have come from being the town drunk, the mayor, the

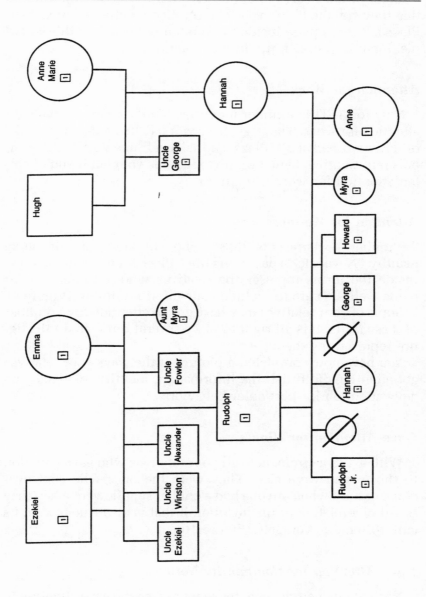

Figure 6. Got Attention for Being Sick

director of the Heart Fund, or a criminal. What is important is that they got attention in the community, whether good or bad. Place a 2 in a square inside the symbol representing those people. Include yourself, if relevant. (Figure 7.)

Attention for Work

Now for 3. This number identifies family members who got attention for work. They may have worked "from dawn to dusk" or never worked at all. Place a 3 inside a frame within the symbols representing them. Be sure to include yourself if you've gotten attention for work. (Figure 8)

Attention for Wellness

Number 4 represents those who got attention for being healthy. "Never sick a day in his life." Place a 4 in a square frame inside the forms representing relatives who got attention for being well. Be sure to include yourself, if it applies. (Figure 9)

Some of your relatives may have gotten attention for a number of these traits. It is all right to place several numbers in the figure representing them.

You have now completed a picture of the ways your relatives got attention. To finish the information, identify relatives who *gave* attention for particular behaviors.

Gave Attention for Illness

With a 1 in a *circle*, note all your relatives who gave attention to those who were sick. They were the ones who sent over chicken soup when anyone had a cold or sent flowers when they heard of a relative in the hospital. If that is also true of you, be sure to include yourself. (Figure 10)

Gave Attention for Community Notice

With a 2 in a circle, note those relatives who gave attention to other family members who received community notice (Figure

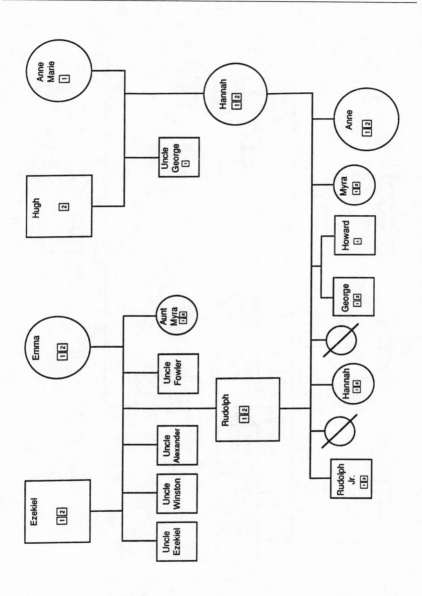

Figure 7. Got Attention for Community Notice

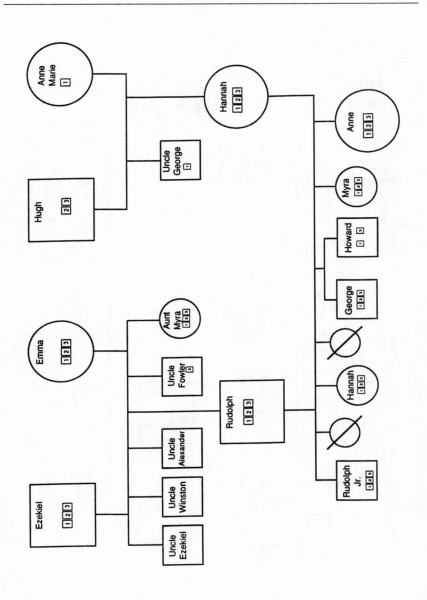

Figure 8. Got Attention for Work

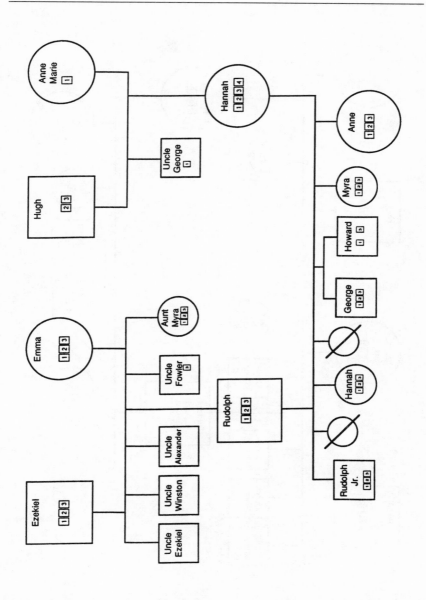

Figure 9. Got Attention for Wellness

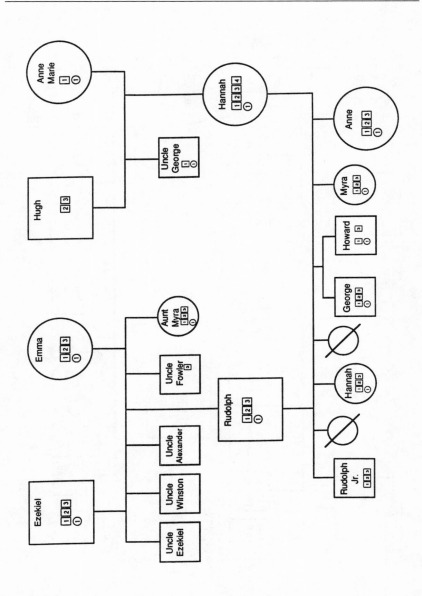

Figure 10. Gave Attention to Those Who Were Sick

11). They may have copied newspaper clippings of any publicity, good or bad, that relatives received and sent them to other members of the family. They may have instigated a party to celebrate the publication of a cousin's book, for example.

Gave Attention for Work

Number 3 in a circle connotes relatives who gave attention for the work others did (Figure 12). It didn't matter whether it was for a great deal of work or none at all. For example, they may have telephoned an unemployed cousin to say that an old family friend was owner of a company that was hiring. They may have been the first to congratulate relatives who were promoted for doing an extraordinary job at work.

Gave Attention for Wellness

Finally, 4 in a circular frame represents those relatives who gave attention to others in the family who were healthy (Figure 13). When my 95-year-old godmother continued to dig her rose garden, we contacted her local newspaper to suggest they interview her, for example.

Now that this part of your genogram is complete, you can ask yourself some questions about your family. The first of these questions will be whether your family had one predominant method of giving and getting attention. Was it by being sick?

By being sick, were members of your family assured of receiving attention? Do you, yourself, regularly give attention to someone who is sick?

Did anyone notice those who were well? Was there any value to being healthy? After all, if no one notices those who are healthy, why continue to go to the effort required to be well?

Do not rush to put the genogram aside. It will give you much information you need to live a healthy life.

Genograms are major sources of guidance in your life. The information they can impart is extremely valuable in predicting your future.

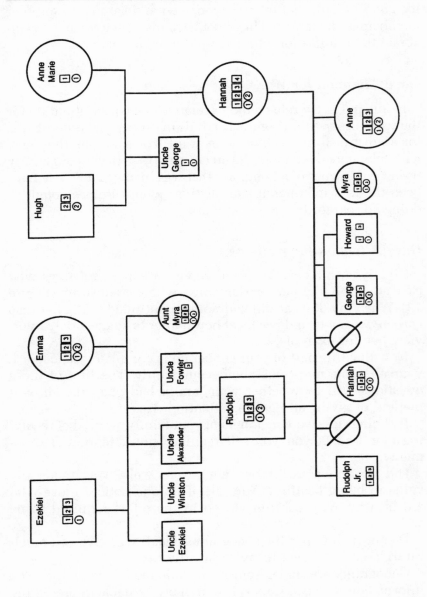

Figure 11. Gave Attention for Community Notice

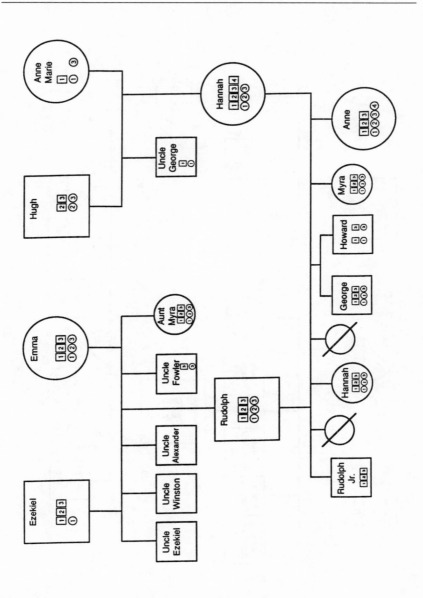

Figure 12. Gave Attention for Work

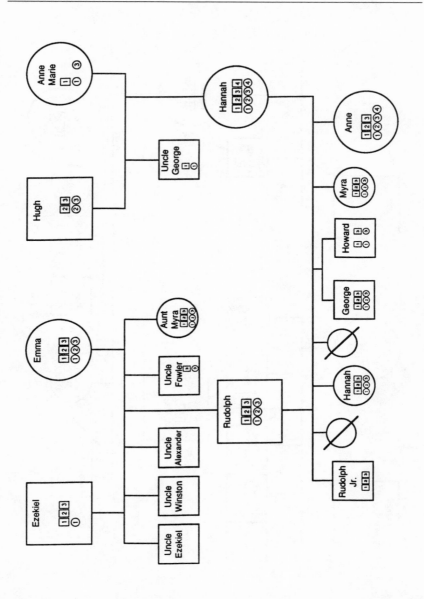

Figure 13. Gave Attention for Wellness

You may learn that the methods of getting and giving attention in your family of origin were quite limited. Those limitations may impede your progress today.

Only women may have served as caretakers in your family. Whenever you, a man, reach out to be compassionate to a family member, you are rebuffed.

It is impossible to change your entire extended family, but maybe you can review your genogram to discover who else is like you. Be in touch with them. Find out how they cope with the power of the family legacy.

Giving Attention

How do you give attention at work? Do you comment on co-workers' successes or failures? Are most of your comments negative?

At home, some people refuse to acknowledge what they like about their significant other. They notice the imperfections, but not the positive traits. Others mention small details.

And then there are the ways we give attention to our kids. Some children are fortunate enough to hear efforts encouraged. Others are constantly scolded for not doing a better job. A former neighbor remarked that as a kid he couldn't get over how my husband and I listened attentively to our children when what they were saying was foolish. In his family, it was necessary to speak sensibly if you were to be heard, regardless of your age.

The way we give attention to our parents is often dependent on how we are encouraged to act by them. After my mother's burial service, my father, then in his 70s, shrugged off my sister's helping him down the church steps. Some parents are happy to receive support, whether emotional, financial, social, or physical, from their children. Others do not want support of any kind. It is important for us to be aware of how we give attention to our parents. Have we found out from them what attention they want, or do we make a unilateral decision on what they need?

Getting Attention

The next question to be addressed is how we get attention.

At a local Pennsylvania hospital, I overheard a woman with cancer tell a nurse, "The only good thing about my illness is that my brother came up from Arizona to see me. We haven't talked for 20 years."

At work, does your supervisor comment on your accomplishments or failures? The clever ideas you have can be invisible or can brighten up your image. If only your failures are recognized, it may be hard to produce enough energy to do a satisfactory job. A question to ask yourself is: "Is work a healing place?"

Your significant other can notice your new outfit or the five pounds you've put on recently. He or she may attend to your physical appearance, but not give attention to your emotional needs.

Your kids, like Vera Kane's in Chapter 4, can notice that you haven't made oatmeal raisin cookies in a long while or that you made their favorite lasagna last week. They may give you flowers and a card on Mother's Day, but fail to accompany you shopping occasionally.

Your parents may tell you that you're a great cook. Or that you're a good storyteller. They may tell you, "Your face is showing a lot of wrinkles." Perhaps they always wait for you to telephone them.

Wants

How do you want to get and give attention? Rather than feeling at the mercy of others' whims, you can take charge of how you get and give attention.

When your daughter complains that you don't buy her enough new clothes, you can refrain from being defensive. For example, you can engage her in discussion that will allow her to expand her ideas on what clothes make her feel part of her peer group.

When your supervisor fails to notice your accomplishments,

you can draw up a chart showing, in living color, the impact of your new marketing program.

If an old friend, who now lives at a distance, telephones when she hears of your sister's death, you can call a few months later to tell her of some happier events.

You can send your father a plant for no reason or send flowers to your significant other on a rainy Monday.

In other words, you have a choice of how you will give and get attention.

Activities

1. What is the overall sense you get from your basic family genogram?
2. What was the main reason for getting attention in your family of origin? Do you still crave attention for that reason?
3. Who were those who gave attention? Was it gender related?
4. What would you like to get attention for at this point in your life?
5. What would you like to give attention for?

3

LIFE DRAWING
Picturing Yourself and
Your Legacy

The new baby lay on her back in the bassinet. She seemed oblivious to all the people hovering over her.

"She looks just like her daddy. She has the same eyes and forehead."

"But her nose and cheeks are definitely Debbie's," an uncle noted.

They all seemed to be scrutinizing the baby with a genetic microscope.

As an adult, you can make a Life Drawing, which shows you what illnesses or maladies you share with your parents.

A Life Drawing requires three things: 1) the help of another person. Enlist the aid of a friend or a family member for five minutes.

2) Large size newsprint, large enough to lie down on.

3) Crayons, at least three of different colors.

THE ACTUAL DRAWING

Lie down on a sheet of newsprint and have your partner outline your form as shown in Figure 14.

Get up and step back from the drawing. With a crayon of a different color, shade all of the sites in which your mother's health

41

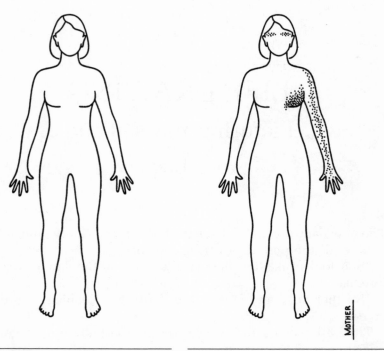

Figure 14. The Self   **Figure 15.** Mother's Health

was imperfect. Be sure to include eye problems, tooth problems, and headaches. They don't have to be calamitous maladies. See Figure 15. Of course, your drawing will be in color.

The drawing indicates the mother's useless left arm (as a result of polio), her left breast cancer, and her poor vision.

Take another crayon and sketch in all of the sites where your father's health was imperfect. Again, include poor vision, tooth problems, headaches, hearing loss. See Figure 16.

The drawing indicates the father's high blood pressure—a light color throughout the body; his lung cancer, hearing problems, and overweight in his abdomen.

At this point, again choose the original color with which

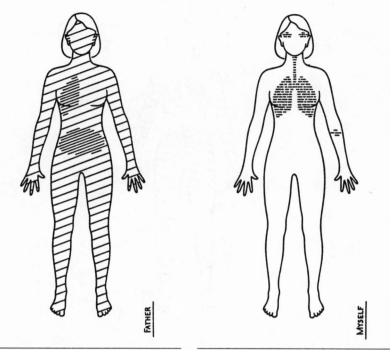

Figure 16. Father's Health   **Figure 17.** Self

your partner drew an outline of your body. That crayon is used to sketch in the imperfections of your own body. See Figure 17.

The sketch shows that you have broken your left arm, cough a good bit from smoking, and have poor vision.

The final drawing will be a composite of the illness sites you share with your parents, as shown in Figure 18.

Your final drawing indicates what sites are vulnerable for you. It shows that you are already having lung problems and weakness in your left arm and in your eyes.

Finally, assess which of the family illnesses can be improved by a lifestyle change.

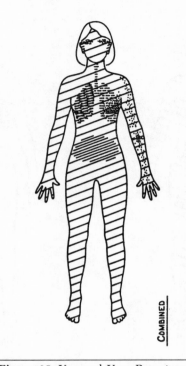

Figure 18. You and Your Parents

CANCELLING

You may want to make a graphic representation that will not have the same faulty organs as your parents. Place an X across that organ in the color that relates to you if you want to keep just one drawing.

Then write a statement of how you want that organ to be. For example, "My eyes are clear and healthy." Write the statement in your own color.

The Life Drawing may be something you want to refer back to periodically in order to see if you are keeping to your own personal design of health.

ACTIVITIES

1. Hang your Life Drawing in a prominent place in your house. It will remind you of the similarities you and your parents share.
2. Bring your Life Drawing with you when you visit your relatives. Get their input about your family's health. My sister and I reminisced about visiting our paternal grandmother. "I always remember her with an onion pinned to her dress," I told Christine. "That was to keep her from getting the flu. Her father died from it," my sister told me.

4

FATALISTS
"It's No Use"

Mary Lou Gustafson, mother of five and in her late 30s, visited me at the behest of her husband. The previous year, Mary Lou's sister had died of breast cancer. Now, Mary Lou had the same illness and expected to suffer the same fate as her sister—death.

When I asked her what she wanted to live for, an important tool of assessment in determining whether a person will survive or not, Mary Lou told me her daughters needed her, but not her sons or husband. There was no personal reason she could give for wanting to live.

About this time, bone scans were performed on Mary Lou to discover if chemotherapy had effectively rid her body of cancer. No cancer appeared on the tests. However, Mary Lou did not feel joyous over those results. She was convinced that she would die.

In fact, two weeks after the negative tests were performed, Mary Lou returned to the cancer hospital, in much pain. Despite new tests that indicated she continued to be free of cancer, Mary Lou remained convinced of her imminent death. She was not persuaded that she could be healthy.

Mary Lou Gustafson was a Fatalist. She did not believe she could change the family health history. She believed she was fated to follow the health outcome of her sister. Her belief was very strong and she continued to hold it up to her death later the same year.

Relative Risks, a book by Nancy C. Baker (1991), notes that women who develop breast cancer expect to receive the same treatment their mothers received 30 years ago, even if that treatment resulted in their parents' death and is no longer used.

Fatalists are people who believe they are helpless to change their family health histories. They frequently believe, like Mary Lou, that they cannot escape it. Without supportive networks, they cannot. And while Mary Lou's friends were supportive, her family felt as fatalistic as she did.

Fatalists are characterized by three traits: 1) a support system that reenforces fatalism; 2) belief that something on the outside determines their fate; 3) belief that the family illness is the "solution" to their problems. They're not surprised if they develop an illness that other members of their family already have had.

The family of Vera Kane, another client of mine, did not support her efforts to change her lifestyle.

NON-SUPPORTIVE FAMILY

Vera is an emergency room nurse—a kind, intelligent, professional woman. She requested therapy to lose weight because her supervisor asserted it was inappropriate for the head of emergency care to be overweight.

Weighing more than is normal for her size is a problem Vera has had since her oldest child was a toddler. At that time, Vera began to put on extra pounds. "To deal with the boredom of being in the house with a kid all the time, I just ate and ate," she explained.

At work, Vera is the picture of professionalism. Her patient charts are up-to-the-minute. Her phone calls are noted with the date and time. The papers on her desk are carefully stacked with precise edges.

Outwardly, all is in order. Except for Vera's size, no sign of inner stress is evident. Like her mother, Vera ranges between 30 and 70 pounds over normal weight.

Vera was concerned that she would be unable to lose the extra pounds on her own. Since no one in her immediate family—her husband, Roy and five adult children—believed her weight was a problem, Vera did not expect them to help her lose weight. She entered therapy to garner support for what she foresaw as a difficult time.

Vera told me that she was born into a poor farm family. Her parents worked seven days a week milking cows, sending the milk to the creamery, making butter, cleaning barn stalls.

After sending two sons to college at great financial sacrifice, Vera's father was surprised that his daughter—"a girl"—wanted more than a high school education. He refused to send her to college. So Vera joined the Army Nurse Corps, which sent her to school.

Vera loved military life and would have made a career of the Army except for meeting Roy Kane, a patient. Roy, a corporal, had wrenched his back lifting heavy equipment that had fallen on one of his buddies.

While reading his hospital chart, Vera discovered that Roy's hometown was several miles from her own. From Roy, she learned that he, too, came from a poor farm family. Unlike her, however, he planned to return home.

Roy and Vera had spirited discussions about living in eastern Pennsylvania. Vera thought the area boring, while Roy considered it very peaceful and beautiful. Talking with each other was the high point of each day for these two shy persons.

When Roy returned to his outfit, Vera missed him. She wrote him long letters describing the daily events in her life and waited for the letters he sent her in return. They arranged to see each other as often as possible.

They were engaged to be married. Vera, now a Captain, followed Roy home several weeks after he was discharged, giving up her career in the military. They planned to be married as soon as possible. Beyond their marriage, nothing was discussed. Not career, family, where to live.

By the time Vera arrived in Pennsylvania, Roy had regained

his job as auto mechanic at a local automobile service station. Vera had no difficulty obtaining a nursing position.

Vera and Roy married. Nine months later Vera gave birth to the first of five children. Vera resigned her nursing job to stay at home and raise her family.

After three years and another child, Vera realized she was starved for mental stimulation. Neither her babies nor her husband provided that. So Vera enrolled in a graduate nursing program. To her delight, she excelled and soon received an offer to become supervisor of the emergency unit in the local hospital.

Although Roy believed that a man's job is to provide for his family, he was persuaded that Vera's salary would provide the family with the extras he could not afford. Primary among those extras was the purchase of a small farm—one of Roy's dreams.

Vera's mother, a widow, cared for her grandchildren during the day while Vera worked in the hospital. After completing her eight-hour shift, Vera would return home and prepare dinner for Roy, her mother, and the two children.

Her mother, 70 pounds overweight and with high blood pressure, died during that time, at age 58.

In the years that followed, Vera gave birth to three more children and continued in the nursing profession. Mother of five, Vera found it was only at work that she was regarded as an intelligent person.

At home, in the small farmhouse Roy had dreamed of, she led the life of a traditional homemaker—homemade oatmeal raisin cookies, clothes air-dried on the washline, handmade quilts on each bed.

When the last child was grown and had moved out of the house, Vera enjoyed the quiet. For the first time since the start of motherhood 25 years before, she and Roy spent time alone. They began to make short visits of two or three days to historic areas.

This period was short-lived.

One by one the grown children reappeared in the lives of their parents. Roy, Jr. returned from a career in finance in New York City because he had a severe car accident that rendered him lame. Clyde's machine shop closed down and he was unable to locate a new job as a machinist. Stanley's marriage disintegrated and he needed a home. Mildred's job as a hairdresser did not pay sufficiently to maintain her own apartment. The youngest, Anna, returned to graduate school.

For all of them, Vera was "helping out for a while" by allowing them to move into the house. As she helped them, her weight increased and her blood pressure soared.

Roy was happy to have his children back; he had missed them. Always a shy homebody, Roy relished the natural commotion that accompanies a houseful of young people and their friends. He was unwilling to take Vera to the movies, church socials, or on vacation since there was enough excitement at home.

Vera became concerned that she was following in her mother's footsteps. As a farmer's wife, Vera's mother had worked hard and received little acknowledgment from her husband for her work accomplishments. Instead, she found that her size did warrant positive attention from her husband, Vera's father. He called her, "My little dumpling."

Like her mother, Vera worked hard and believed there was no relief in sight. She overate since there was no other pleasure she could grant herself. Like her father, Vera's husband made endearing comments about his wife's size.

At my encouragement, Vera began swimming at the local YWCA several times a week. She found a friend to swim with her and share an occasional outing to a movie. She attended a class in meditation.

After Vera had reestablished some of her positive feelings about herself, she lost weight naturally.

As she succeeded in developing a better self-image, Vera reported some of the objections her family made about her new behaviors. "Tell that doctor (the internist who said that adult children should live on their own) to mind his own business." "You're out too much." "You didn't even make any cookies this week." "Who's going to iron my shirts?" "Nothing seems to bother you anymore." "Maybe you have anorexia."

In spite of having to make changes against her family's will, Vera's blood pressure returned to normal and her weight slowly descended. It was then that she told me how hard it would be to continue to resist her family. Her husband was particularly critical of her "selfish" attitudes. He considered her consciousness about herself—her weight and her happiness—to be inconsiderate of the family. Devoutly religious, Vera believed her first obligation was towards her family. She believed, further, that she should follow her husband's dictates.

In her nuclear family, it was impossible to follow a healthy lifestyle. She said, "I'm blossoming, but no one likes my blossoms." Vera did not want to create "waves" at home. She left therapy, fully convinced she could not maintain the changes she had accomplished without her family's help.

Vera is a good example of a Fatalist. She did not believe personal changes could make a difference in her life. She was a victim of family influence. Vera wanted her family to enjoy and support her new lifestyle. Her unwillingness to utilize support from friends and her inability to demand it from her family resulted in Vera's giving up on herself. Despite her wish not to follow in her mother's footsteps, she felt doomed to have poor health without her family's support. In the end she succumbed to the myth—that one is powerless in the face of family illness.

SUPPORT SYSTEM

Vera was right in thinking she needed a support system. The support didn't have to come from her family, though. She could have used her friends' help and interest in her more than she did.

Often, friends urge you to continue a course of lifestyle change that your family may not support. Friends may have more faith that you can be different than your family does. They are somewhat more objective about you than your family is.

Friends may encourage you to discontinue living as you have. Another source of support may be from a therapist or from a church-related group.

Therapy for the grief that ensues after a diagnosis of chronic illness is helpful, but many people feel that they just want to forget the whole thing. They do not want to pursue therapy where they will be urged to reveal their feelings about the new realities facing them. Others, who seek support while they are attempting to follow a more healthful lifestyle, are embarrassed to admit that they need help to stop smoking, to attend the gym, to pursue a new eating regime, or to practice stress management.

Those who leave therapy before it is completed are commonly those who feel destined to live the life they are living. They feel helpless to alter their behavior. In fact, some say that if they had power to alter their behavior their families would no longer love them. Being loved is more important to them than being well. They do not believe that those who love them will continue to do so if they change.

THERAPY

Because few Fatalists actively seek therapy, I rarely have a chance to work with them. They usually think, "Therapy is a crock," or "Only crazy people go into therapy." As one man who completed a health questionnaire for me said, "This is a bunch of hokum."

Some Fatalists I have worked with sought therapy for a cause other than their health. The health issue surfaced as we worked on other issues. Other Fatalists entered therapy because someone told them they should.

Phyllis and Harry Chesney sought therapy for marital problems. Phyllis complained that Harry seldom entered into lively discussions with her except on long drives to visit her parents.

Harry expressed frustration with Phyllis's complaints and told her he loved her deeply.

In developing a genogram, Phyllis spoke of her childhood in the city and Harry of his on a farm. It was then that Phyllis learned of Harry's hearing loss. Using farm machinery as an adolescent, Harry lost normal hearing. His parents didn't seek help for him as they refused to accept responsibility for any of his problems. They saw such acceptance as admitting blame for the problem.

Harry had inherited the belief that if he sought help for himself, he was blaming his parents for his hearing loss. He did not want to blame and hurt them.

When Harry was in the confines of a small car with Phyllis, he had less difficulty hearing her. Their conversations at that time were intimate. However, when they were at home, the noises of the dishwasher, clothes dryer, television, and refrigerator interfered with Harry's ability to hear his soft-spoken wife.

Phyllis urged her husband to reclaim his personal power and discontinue life as a Fatalist. She helped him visit an ear specialist where Harry learned that he was totally deaf in one ear. When he first began to use a hearing aid, Harry was skeptical that it could cause any major change in his life.

After wearing a hearing aid for a short time, Harry was amazed at how much his attitude toward life's challenges had changed. He didn't feel helpless anymore.

HELPLESSNESS

Dr. Martin E.P. Seligman at the University of Pennsylvania (1991) has researched the issue of helplessness in persons with a fatal illness. He found that the poorer their "explanatory style" the more likely patients are to have serious illnesses. Patients who are depressive, negativistic, or pessimistic about life events also possess those attitudes about health. They accept serious ill health with an air of helplessness and feel it is up to health practitioners to produce good health again. They are unable to develop lifestyle changes that can alter their health themselves.

Families who have a powerless attitude toward health model a lifestyle of helplessness.

A person who smokes and is a member of a family having lots of heart disease is a Fatalist. That person refuses to believe personal efforts can overcome his or her tendency to be vulnerable to the family illness.

The self-destructive behavior of Fatalists—like smoking,

being overweight, having a stressful work life—is not seen by them as controllable. They say things like, "You got to die of something."

And of course you do. Agreeing with the idea "Eat, drink, and be merry, for tomorrow we die" seems reasonable. It is true.

The notion that enjoying life is somehow sinful is also accepted by some persons.

PUNISHMENT FOR SIN

Many religious people believe that illness is God's punishment for sin. Thus, when a family member becomes ill, their compassion is tinged with the belief that in some way the ill person deserved to suffer the malady. That attitude deprives the sick person of comfort and support. The one who is sick not only suffers with the illness, but also is burdened with the belief that somehow he or she deserves the illness as a punishment from God.

Michael Reilly, a close family friend, developed lung cancer in his 40s. Michael had been a longtime smoker who had recently stopped his habit.

When faced with his diagnosis, Michael resigned himself to being the recipient of either a miracle or death. He believed that either outcome was beyond his control. God would decide which result would develop. Michael was powerless.

At a healing meeting in his church, Michael's sister noticed that no one touched her brother. When she asked why that was so, she was told, "He has cancer, you know." There was a belief that cancer is unholy and the unholiness that existed in the sick person's body could invade the other bodies that came in contact with the malady.

During the last weeks of Michael's life, his best friend told me Michael said he was waiting for a miracle.

I asked Michael at that time what he looked forward to. His answer, "I'll write you a letter," sent a cold shiver through me. I felt it indicated he had no future goals. His life ended before he ever wrote me the letter.

In order for Michael Reilly to accept the belief that chemo-therapy could alter the course of his illness, the religious coun-selors he consulted would have had to strongly believe in God's perfection. However, they, too, were Fatalists and believed God allowed events, both good and evil, to unfold. I believe their understanding of God was flawed. While they did not state that God also created ill health, their belief system showed that they accepted this concept.

Michael Reilly could have been supported by a basic religious belief—that everything created by God is perfect. And while his tumor was a perfect creation, it was destroying another perfect creation of God—Michael. Since chemotherapy was ultimately created by God, it could successfully overcome the destructive-ness of the tumor so that Michael could continue to live.

Trying to regain good health when one is ill requires future hopes. Without them, the difficult work of recovery oftentimes becomes too burdensome. And Fatalists don't have future hopes.

FUTURE HOPES

Those who have grown up without future hopes do not know how to develop them. Religious people may say that they are fol-lowing God's plan for them. They wait, like St. Paul, for a momentous display of God's guidance. Without a miracle, what can they do?

Many children, who have parameters drawn around their lives by school schedules, thrive. Few adults have any personal deadlines in their lives. The reason many of them suffer from "The Empty Nest Syndrome" or "Mid-Life Crisis" or confusion about retirement plans is that no outside authority designates what a person is to do with that time of life.

Often, during the time after children have left home, their par-ents do not know what to do with themselves. Frequently, they exhort their grown children to marry and have babies so they can continue their roles of care and nurturance.

In mid-life, some adults, particularly men, recreate an earlier time of their lives, typically adolescence. They leave a field they have worked in for a long time, dissolve a marriage, begin dressing differently, develop relationships with younger people.

When retirement looms, some people refuse to make any plans for retirement years. They conceive of themselves as only workers.

To develop future hopes, it helps to keep a collection of essays concerning older people. Do you love the story of Grandma Moses beginning to paint at 84? Or that Kitty Carlisle Hart made her debut in New York City at 54? Or that George Burns has contracts to appear in London in his hundredth year?

It might help to post a picture of your idol on your refrigerator or the back of your bathroom door—a place where you can see it each day.

Whom do you want to emulate? You can "program" yourself to live the life that appeals to you.

Oncologist Carl Simonton, M.D. and associates, in the book *Getting Well Again* (1978), state that recovery from cancer is unlikely without hopes for the future. While Michael Reilly dutifully took the medicine given him, he had no strong desire to attain any personal goals.

Many adults do not routinely set up future hopes for themselves. They live from one day to the next with no day seeming special. All days are the same.

At this moment, do you remember what you wore to work two days ago? What did you eat for dinner last night? What are you looking forward to?

To give yourself excuses for not carrying out your personal dreams is easy. You can tell yourself you would have a better wardrobe if you had somewhere to go. Your apartment would be nicer if you had a roommate to share expenses with you. You would have a family if your spouse didn't object to being a parent.

In what ways do you sabotage yourself from achieving your goals? If you get sick, those same behaviors will thwart your efforts to return to good health.

Fatalists are usually good at providing themselves with reasons why they can't attain objectives.

Concerning health, they may say, "My case is different." "The doctor says I can never have a baby."

The very notion of setting goals for good health is antithetical to being a Fatalist. Yet, many Fatalists succeed in the business world where setting work goals is common practice. They acknowledge the effectiveness of goalsetting in business—it increases revenue and motivates staff. Yet those same people rarely translate effective, work-related techniques into their personal lives.

Promising to give up cigarettes "one of these days" with no firm deadline for cessation is a common stance taken by Fatalists. So is deciding, "Stress never ends." Going on a diet "Monday" instead of this minute is another habit of Fatalists.

Expecting fate to remedy what they have failed to do is easier than making health goals for their future.

Vera Kane expects to inherit the physical problems of her mother's side of the family. Changing her belief in the myth of her powerlessness might help her change her lifestyle and aid her in living a longer, healthier life.

PROGRAMMING

Patricia Murphy, a 38-year-old executive secretary, is an example of an individual "programmed" to carry out a family legacy of illness. Patricia offered to talk with me after she had suffered a heart attack. Like other Fatalists who seek the latest and best treatment sources, Patricia saw a group of cardiologists at a high-tech hospital. She had already been interviewed by a research group of a medical school before I saw her. One of her team of cardiologists told her the heart attack she suffered was caused by a hereditary problem and advised her that nothing she did would have any effect on her future health. Patricia did not question his expertise. In her mind, there was no connection between her lifestyle and her health. She believed she was helpless to effect any change in her health.

She continued to smoke, remain overweight, eat junk food, and experience stress from her job and the political activities she engaged in. Her young children, ages 8 and 11, saw her living an unhealthy lifestyle, just as Patricia had watched her father. He had died of a heart attack at 40.

Her mother told the young Patricia that she was just like her father. She further declared that Patricia's brother was just like her. Now in her seventies, Patricia's mother continues in good health, as does her 36-year-old son. Both of them jog daily, eat a nutritious diet, don't smoke, and manage stress well.

Although a well-educated woman, Patricia does not question fate. She learned early and well that she was destined to die young of a heart attack and that is what she expects to happen.

The fact that she does nothing to change her lifestyle and to program her children differently from the way she was programmed does not occur to her.

Recently, at the urging of her employer, she visited a Naturopath, an expert in vitamins, minerals, and the natural healing of the body. She was advised by this outside expert to change her diet. She did so. For the first time in nearly a year, she is free of pain. Patricia now questions some of the beliefs she was taught.

She questioned her cardiologist about his original advice that she could do nothing to improve her health. "New studies show that giving up smoking, losing weight, and exercising will help you." he said. In fact Dean Ornish, M.D.'s (1990) program in California showed that not only can such techniques help but they can even reverse heart damage.

Developing future hopes is an experience she has not had. Whether she will change from being a Fatalist to being a Fighter is still a question.

CARETAKERS

Patients who fail to have goals for the future often frustrate their caretakers. The caretakers seem more determined that the patient return to good health than the patient is. Without patient motivation, the best care is often useless.

Caretakers must realize that it is the responsibility of the patient to develop future goals. The caretakers' goals and the patients' may not match.

That was the situation in Charlotte Richards' home.

Charlotte Richards' brother and sister-in-law were seeing me for marital therapy when they suggested to Charlotte that she consult me about the affair she was having with a married man, her boss.

Charlotte was 20 years old. Six months previously, she had undergone cancer surgery. She was not concerned about cancer reoccurring, however. She was concerned about the man she loved and how soon he would leave his wife and children to marry her. Her thoughts always returned to him.

Her lover told her he couldn't divorce his wife because his three children were very young. Charlotte was disappointed they could not marry, but resolved to wait until they could. Simultaneously with her decision to wait, the remission of her cancer ended.

Charlotte and I discussed the possible physiological benefits that ending the affair might have on her health and she told me that even if it meant recovering her health, she would never leave Albert. She preferred to be terminally ill to ending her relationship with him. She was obsessed with his good looks and the attention he paid her.

She felt she could not share the facts of her love life with her parents, who, she feared, would be "horrified" by her actions. Because the affair was secret, Charlotte had given up all social life. While there were many people who knew of or suspected Charlotte's affair, it was not known publicly, so spending time with friends was impossible. The only people Charlotte told of her relationship with Albert were her brother and his wife.

Charlotte ended therapy when she recognized that discussing choices upset her. As a Fatalist, she felt helpless to make choices about her future and did not want to be reminded that she had other options.

From her brother, I later learned that Charlotte's cancer had progressed until she could no longer maintain her own apartment. She moved into her parents' house, where her lover visited her in the guise of a concerned boss. Because Charlotte was so ill, her parents did not deprive her of anything, least of all visits from her boss.

As her caretakers, her parents drove Charlotte to New York City's Sloan-Kettering Hospital from eastern Pennsylvania for chemotherapy treatments and turned their living room into a sickroom. My clients, Charlotte's brother and sister-in-law, asked me to conduct a therapy session with the entire family at Charlotte's parents' home. Charlotte's brother was very concerned about his mother's health. He was fearful that his mother's constant care of Charlotte was undermining her own health.

When I arrived at the house, I saw that Charlotte's medical accoutrements—suction machine, oxygen tank—dominated the room. Charlotte commandeered the couch in a long white nightgown and robe, her waist-length black hair brushed into a bun at the back of her neck, her large brown eyes peering out of her ghostly white, flawless face.

Mrs. Richards was totally devoted to her daughter's health. She was afraid to leave the house to shop, attend church, or visit friends. Even with a professional nurse in the house, Mrs. Richards feared that her daughter would die while she was away from home.

My suggestion to use a beeper so that Mrs. Richards could be summoned by a nurse if she went to the store or to church went unheeded. Charlotte did not ask her mother to follow my advice. Rather, Charlotte told her, "If it makes you more comfortable to be here with me all the time, I guess you'll have to do that."

In spite of the urging by her son and daughter-in-law and her husband to get some outside relief, Mrs. Richards stayed with her daughter, night and day.

As a young mother, Mrs. Richards had taken care of her children when her own mother was ill with cancer. She believed her responsibility was to take care of her new family. After her mother died, however, she felt guilty that she hadn't nursed her mother herself. She believed that if she had, her mother would have lived longer.

With Charlotte's health declining rapidly, her mother was determined to be with her constantly. She expected Charlotte to regain her health, despite the fact that Charlotte did not share those expectations. Charlotte believed in the inevitability of death from cancer and that she was fated to follow in the footsteps of her dead grandmother.

Throughout Charlotte's illness, Mrs. Richards remained available to her. She was with her when she died one winter night.

The goals of Charlotte and of her primary caretakers were not the same. Charlotte wished for marriage to her unavailable boss. Her mother wanted her daughter to regain her health, but to rely on her totally. Her father acted as if all choices were out of his hands. The brother and sister-in-law who sought my help wanted Charlotte to face reality—give up her lover, regain her health, move away from her parents. None of the goals matched.

SEXUAL PROBLEMS

Another family whose goals were mismatched was that of Rachel Epstein, another former client. Rachel was an accomplished social studies teacher. She and her husband, Edward, sought therapy for sexual problems.

After undergoing a mastectomy, Rachel was hurt by Edward's obvious revulsion regarding her appearance. He refused to have sex with the light on, for example. He encouraged her to have breast reconstruction, not for her sake but for his. He indicated she "would look more appealing to him."

While Rachel was willing to undergo breast reconstruction, she felt that Edward was not supportive of her for her own sake. "He only wants me to look better for him."

Despite her feelings, Rachel underwent reconstructive surgery and Edward resumed his sexual interest in her. They subsequently embarked on a tour of cancer groups to discuss the benefits of reconstructive breast surgery.

Edward enjoyed openly talking about sex to groups of other couples. It gave him a forum to discuss his feelings. After an interval, Rachel began to resent what she considered an intrusion into her privacy. Sex problems again surfaced—Rachel's resistance to her husband's sexual overtures and Edward's anger that his wife was "uninterested" in sex. It was then that the couple sought marital therapy.

Rachel had a family history of women not interested in sex who died early in life from the complications of breast cancer.

Both Rachel's mother and aunt had had breast cancer. Rachel was aware that some studies show that the disease has a hereditary component, but is also affected by behavioral habits. She concluded that she was following the behavior of her mother and aunt.

Her father was a prominent physician who liked to parade his wife in front of his colleagues in the clothes and jewels he bought her. There was little intimacy between them. Sex was a ritual that Rachel's mother felt required to perform. She once told her daughter she viewed intercourse "like brushing my teeth."

Her mother's sister, Sophie, had also married a financially successful man. She, too, wore the outward signs of success in her milieu—furs and jewels. Like her sister, Sophie reported dissatisfaction with sex.

Rachel felt helpless concerning her husband. She believed it was impossible to leave her teenaged daughter a different legacy than the one given her by her mother and aunt. She was reliving old tapes. She, too, was only a symbol of her husband's success as her mother and aunt were. They were not appreciated for themselves.

About a year after active breast cancer had gone into remission, Rachel was diagnosed as having bone cancer.

After treatment, Rachel returned to her teaching job. She said emphatically that if living with her husband meant a return of cancer and inevitable death, she felt doomed to accept the inevitable. She refused to consider further changes she and Edward needed to make. She surrendered to her fate.

The myth of being helpless to redesign family health history influenced Rachel. She did not believe she could thrive by changing her lifestyle. She followed the script of the women before her in every way, including having and dying from breast cancer.

COMMONALITIES

Charlotte and Rachel were only two of many who told me they would sooner die than give up a relationship. They were unhappy in the relationship, but felt helpless to end it. When they developed a fatal illness, the illness created a way out. A way out that appeared beyond the control of the sick person. "The family illness can be a solution to a problem that is not considered solvable," Rachel told me. When families teach members that certain issues have only one solution—death—the members know no other options to use when faced with a serious problem.

In the past, the solution to marital problems was often to have a baby. For some people, terminal illness has become a similar solution.

It is not that people consciously choose to be terminally ill. But, as Fatalists, they rarely take measures that result in good health. They merely follow the family script laid out for them.

OUT OF BALANCE

Gertrude Babbitt followed the family script also.

The first time Gertrude entered my second-floor office, she struggled to climb the steps. Gertrude was suffering from advanced osteoporosis and used a cane to walk. Because of her difficulty, we later met at her home.

Through the dining room window, we could see a pond and an egret standing on one leg. The egret reminded Gertrude of a time when she was an excellent dancer and acrobat. Her eyes filled with tears as she told me of her former flexible body. She told me of the changes her illness had caused.

Gertrude needed to have someone buy groceries for her as she could not walk the long aisles of the food market. She could not attend church because the building had a long flight of unbanistered steps leading to it. Visiting friends was difficult, and even shopping for shoes or a blouse required more effort than she felt able to expend. She had been a star tennis player and no longer played. She refused to visit the courts to watch friends play the game, as watching simply frustrated her.

Gertrude was aware that osteoporosis ran in her family. Both her mother and first cousin suffered from it. She regularly drank milk, ate cheese, and kept herself physically active. It wasn't until the year her 92-year-old father entered a nursing home and her only son married a drug addict that Gertrude showed any signs of developing the illness. She was 48 years old.

An only child, Gertrude was very close to her father. He had been widowed at an early age by his wife's death from the complications of osteoporosis. Gertrude often spent time with her father, particularly when her husband was away on business. When the elderly man became incapacitated, his loss to her was devastating.

Her husband was a lawyer who was totally involved in his work. He frequently travelled internationally and made no changes in his interesting work because of Gertrude's illness. He continued to live the independent life he had grown accustomed to in his marriage.

About the same time, Gertrude's brilliant, college-educated son became engaged to a teenaged girl who was actively involved in the use of drugs. Gertrude believed that if she continued to resist her son's determination to marry and to love his girlfriend into drug-free health, he would not marry her. Instead, her son totally distanced himself from his mother and married the girl. He and his wife did not visit her, nor did they even telephone.

Gertrude began having trouble walking after her father moved to a nursing home and her son married. Soon she used a walker and utilized friends to do her food shopping and laundry. The pain she experienced was constant, with intermittent stronger levels of intensity.

Gertrude received medical treatment that embraced the most advanced technology on osteoporosis. Nonetheless, she believed her condition would progressively worsen. She expected a bleak and brief future just as her mother had experienced.

With the help of therapy, Gertrude reestablished contact with her son.

Despite this success, Gertrude continued to believe there was no hope that she could regain her health. "It's inevitable."

Always slim, Gertrude gained 30 pounds from medication and inactivity; she no longer was proud of her body. In fact, she peppered her conversation with derogatory comments about her looks, calling herself "a doddering fat lady." At 52, Gertrude saw no light at the end of the tunnel.

She was able to create mental imagery to diminish her pain. (Mental imagery is a form of self-hypnosis that helps people visualize what they would like to attain. It will be described further in Chapter 5.) My suggestion that she could use the same technique to stem the spread of osteoporosis was met with disbelief and non-compliance.

Gertrude was a Fatalist in selected parts of her life, especially as concerned her health. She did not believe her life could be a fulfilling, healthy one. She believed it was impossible to become well and that the best medical care as well as personal insight into her behavioral habits could not successfully reverse her disease. She ended therapy. I telephoned her twice to offer further work, but Gertrude refused. A few months later, I learned of her death.

Gertrude did not believe she could overcome the myth of family illness. She thought she was powerless to change the family legacy.

You cannot attain success without believing in your ability to do so. Belief alone is insufficient to turn illness around, but added to medical treatment it can be a very powerful tool to aid recovery.

FAMILY SCRIPT

You may learn as a child that you are likely to get heart disease, for example. Even though the most frequent cause of death in the United States is heart disease, few types of heart disease have proven to be hereditary. (See Appendix II.) However, heart disease does "run in families. " Whether or not one can totally eliminate the possibility of developing heart disease by following a healthy lifestyle is not yet known. But a "heart-healthy" lifestyle does minimize your chances of having heart disease.

Another person who felt powerless to refuse the family script is Bill Merit, a college professor of mine. Bill believes that fate is stronger than any effort he may exert to be healthy. When his son, Bill, Jr., asked him about the cause of death of his grandfather and great-grandfather, Bill told him both men had died at age 63 of heart attacks.

"If your father died at 63 and his father died at 63 and if you die at 63, does that mean I have to do the same?," Bill, Jr. asked his father.

Bill, Jr. is the apple of his father's eye. He is a tall, gangly 14-year-old who plays soccer.

It was not easy for Bill to dismiss his concern.

Gloria, Bill's wife, has ceased urging her husband to lose weight, stop smoking, and "cheer up." Her urging simply causes arguments between them.

A history professor, Bill encourages his students to analyze why world societies declare war on one another. "What we don't learn from history, we are doomed to repeat," Bill often tells his classes.

Yet he fails to exercise, to stop smoking, to lose 50 pounds, to laugh more. The periodic bouts of depression he experiences are handled by a trip to his physician, who prescribes a tranquillizer and hustles him out of his office with a pat on the back and a casual, "Take it easy."

And that is how Bill reacts. He takes it all very casually.

SKEPTICS

A subtler kind of Fatalist is the Skeptic who seems to ignore the family legacy. While Skeptics practice good health habits, they don't necessarily believe they will be successful ultimately.

Skeptics don't believe, for example, that being slim, not smoking, jogging daily, or eating well will override the family legacy of high blood pressure. They believe that an improved lifestyle might postpone the family illness, but won't eliminate it.

They ask themselves what good practicing healthy habits will be if they won't succeed anyhow. A lot of time and work is expended for little reward. If you're going to die young after all, they reason, why go to the effort of giving up smoking, jogging in the rain, eliminating sugar and salt from your diet?

Getting the family illness is not the worst legacy. The fear of getting it is. Spending years of one's life worrying about getting heart disease or cancer is criminal. You can't enjoy your good health when you are worried about inevitably getting sick. Nor can you enjoy recovery when such recovery is not considered indicative of further good health.

If you have suffered from a cold once, you do not say you are in remission from colds when you are well. However, if you have had a heart attack or cancer, everyone looks at you and you look at yourself as in remission. Neither the medical profession or you, yourself, see you as well.

Skeptics can sometimes "smell the coffee." They are more open to learning new methods of behavior. They can be turned around—to develop awareness of their motivations for health. For them, changing a physical lifestyle has usually been done already. What needs to be changed is their attitude toward being powerful personally.

AN ATTITUDE OF INEVITABILITY

A participant at one of my illness workshops, Beth James (as cited in chapter 1), has a doom-laden attitude about health. Beth is an energetic 34-year- old financial analyst, the picture of robust good health. She jogs, eats a healthy diet, stays slim, doesn't smoke, meditates, keeps her stress level in check. Nonetheless, Beth fears that her efforts will probably be in vain because of her family history.

At the workshop, Beth drew a lifesize replica of herself, a Life

Drawing as described in Chapter 3, with her parents' and her own illnesses noted within it. "It's inevitable. I'll get hypertension from my mother's side or heart disease from my father's. I was always the maverick. And if I don't follow one side or the other of my family, I'll never be accepted."

The other seminar participants were aghast at Beth's comment. Yet she expressed what many people believe but do not say. She believed she had to develop one of the family illnesses. Not doing so "would be the last straw."

She recognizes that hypertension and many heart diseases have not been proven to be hereditary. Using salt, being under constant stress, being overweight are all factors identified in the development of hypertension. Some heart diseases have a hereditary component, while others are environmentally produced. Yet Beth believes that it is inevitable that she inherit one disease or another from her family of origin.

Beth's life has been overshadowed by the myth of family illness. Her belief that she is powerless to change her future has a strong impact on her. She has accepted the family legacy without making a choice about wanting it or not.

Some people with a family history of illness find it difficult to practice good health habits. After all, why go to the trouble when their efforts will probably prove useless?

The reason for following healthy habits is that because there is disagreement about what percentage of illness is genetic, following a healthy lifestyle may result in a long and healthy life. It is a mistake to feel destined to develop the family illness and die from it.

Even illnesses that hold higher rates of probability need not doom us.

FAMOUS FATALISTS

We often read in the biographies of celebrities that they inherit the lifestyle of a parent.

Steve McQueen, the actor who died of cancer in 1989 at age 50, was a Fatalist. His ex-wife, Neile, quotes him as saying, "I'm gonna die young, so I gotta take a big piece out of life." His mother had died young, also. (Spiegel, 1986)

Another well-known Fatalist was Jim Fixx, the jogging advocate. His father suffered his first heart attack at age 35 and succumbed to heart disease eight years later.

At age 35, Jim Fixx began jogging, but told his wife he knew he would die young.

Although he began a national craze, jogging, Fixx continued to believe he was doomed to follow in the tragic footsteps of his father.

He refused to undergo a stress test. A few years later, he collapsed while jogging and died at the age of 52. (New York Times, 1984).

Elvis Presley, another Fatalist, believed in "the way of things." As a youngster, he was a member of a Southern fundamentalist church where belief in God's retribution was strong. Sin was punished. Before her death, his mother, Gladys, was very upset by reports in national magazines that her son's music was the work of the devil and corrupting the nation's youth (Dundy, 1985). Before his own death, Elvis was very upset over the publication of a book by two of his former bodyguards about his drug addiction and disrespect for anything but himself. (West, West & Hebler, 1977).

Like his mother, Elvis brooded about disappointments. Such stress influenced his health. He did nothing to avoid following in his mother's health footsteps. He ate too much and binged on junk food. He took a variety of drugs for insomnia, stress, weight loss, and hypertension. He no longer exercised.

Elvis was indeed a Fatalist, one who believes whatever happens is inevitable.

UNKNOWN FATALISTS

Each of the persons described in this chapter believed they were doomed to develop a physical problem that had previously occurred in their families. When they became ill, they were not surprised. It was only after I asked specific questions about their lifestyles that each realized that he or she had repeated the lifestyle of relatives who had had the same malady. They did not believe that it was possible to change their fate by changing their lifestyles. They felt powerless.

It is helpful to ask yourself these specific questions:

Do I look like relatives who died young? You may be over-weight as they were, have the same nicotine-stained fingers, have pallid skin.

Do I smoke as much as relatives who died young?

Am I as given to sayings used by early-dying relatives? Do I say the same things they often said? For example, "It'll get you in the end," or "You'll never get out of life alive."

Do I know the latest treatment and diagnostic tests for the "family illness?"

Feeling helpless is one of the hallmarks of being a Fatalist. Yet you can still reclaim your power, if you feel helpless. Following are some activities designed to aid you in changing:

ACTIVITIES

1. On the family genogram you constructed, add what illnesses caused the deaths of your relatives. Ask older members of your family for the answers you do not know. Some illnesses, such as your grandmother's "women's problems," can only be guessed at.
2. Notice how often you say, "I can't help it," "That's the way it is," "All us Joneses (put in your family name) get heart disease (or whatever the family illness is)." Eliminate those sayings from your repertoire.

5

FIGHTERS
"I Make My Own Future"

Robin Clay, an engineer, spoke to me about his family's health history. His father died at 40 of a heart attack. His sister had already suffered a heart attack at 38.

While Robin's wife is alarmed by her sister-in-law's health, Robin is confident he will not follow in the footsteps of his father and sister.

Unlike them, he does not smoke nor is he overweight. Robin runs every day, eats a diet low in fats—and he sails, skis, and swims in the appropriate seasons.

He has an annual physical to make certain his cholesterol level is low and his heart is healthy. He even has directed his children's pediatrician to check their cholesterol levels and include a more rigid heart exam than is usually given healthy children.

Robin believes that he can teach his children a healthy lifestyle. He refuses to be a victim of biological determinism. Unlike the model he received from his father, Robin has decided to provide his children with a healthy father figure.

Fighters, like Robin, voluntarily disinherit themselves of the family legacy of early death and illness. Despite common family occurrences of chronic illness or premature deaths, they follow lifestyles likely to keep them well. They do not smoke. They are not "couch potatoes." They practice stress management techniques and eat low-fat diets.

SAYING "NO"

Eugenia Otis, a former client, is also an example of a Fighter, a person who refuses the family legacy of early death and illness. Eugenia, a retired school teacher in her early 60s, discovered a lump in her breast that was diagnosed as cancer. A religious woman, she initially accepted the illness as "God's will." However, she believed she was ethically required to follow medical advice focused on recovery.

Her usual boundless energy was curtailed by the chemotherapy treatments prescribed. Such lack of energy made it simpler for her to say "No" to invitations to serve on various church and community boards. It was after the cancer treatments were completed that Eugenia found it difficult to say "No" for her own sake.

We explored what she called "feelings of selfishness." She remembered that, as a child, whenever she wanted to do something for herself, either her father, a minister, or her mother, a "proper" minister's wife, told her she was being selfish and displeasing God. The eldest of four children, Eugenia was very serious about accepting "God's will." Being in tune with "God's plan" meant that Eugenia had to follow a lifestyle of selflessness.

About the time Eugenia was undergoing chemotherapy treatment, a young minister she met told her, "God helps those who help themselves." This was a new way of thinking for Eugenia. It was a more powerful explanation of God's plan and a less passive stance for a physically ill person, like her, to emulate.

"If I can accept 'God's will' to be sick, there's no reason I can't accept that God wants me to do all I can to be well," she told me.

Embracing that attitude, Eugenia began to take piano and painting lessons, something she had wanted to do all her life. She found that she could spend time painting or practicing piano without feeling she was being selfish. She could refuse to serve on various committees because she knew that making other people's needs the Number One priority in her life resulted in obscuring her own needs for spiritual development. A new feeling of self-worth developed for Eugenia.

After she had no active cancer for seven years, Eugenia offered to take her 13-year-old granddaughter on a trip to Europe. It was a festive trip for her. A celebration of life.

Eugenia Otis's former belief was that relying on oneself to regain good health rather than relying totally on God for help is somehow irreligious. There are others who believe the same thing. They think that to be well, they must only pray to God for good health. When their prayers are not answered, they say that their prayers were flawed or that God wants them to be ill for some reason.

A number of parents who rely on prayer rather than immunizing their children against illnesses have had to fight the legal system which requires immunization before a child is allowed to attend public school. Their belief that God will protect their children from illness is scoffed at by others in the society who argue that immunization of all children decreases the risk to others. But to those who believe in God's power, belief in medicine somehow minimizes His power. It is sacrilegious.

There are those who do not believe that their bodies are a gift of God and need to be cared for as a God-given treasure. Instead they believe that God lends us a body, but continues to hold possession of it. They make God responsible for the body's health— like a landlord who is responsible to fix the hot water heater.

Fighters do all they can to reclaim the power of a healthy body. They do not believe that God experiences any hesitation about their taking good care of the gift He gave them—a healthy body.

In fact the idea that God would not support their efforts is foreign to them. There is controversy, however, about whether God gives people illness to learn something—a sort of Job experience, as in the Bible story. Believers in such theory feel they need to have the illness in order to learn a truth they've been avoiding.

Others, myself included, believe that illness arrives only after we have failed to receive other more gentle messages. Our families have trained us to minimize gentle messages. We await something dramatic, such as severe chest pain, before we respond.

When a baby cries because he or she is hungry, the baby is not ignored because nearby adults believe the baby needs to learn about hunger. Yet some adults believe God wills them to accept poor health and not seek expert help to remedy it.

BIBLICAL INJUNCTIONS

Using quotations taken from the Old and New Testaments of the Bible, adherents of these beliefs have been deeply programmed to believe that what went before is destined to be repeated.

"Let his blood be on me and on my children."

"A plague be on your household."

The question is how one follows one's religion and at the same time does not feel guilty for being healthy.

Is being healthy a state we can control? Or does God control our health? A few stories from the Bible elucidate our heritage of belief in miracles.

The intervention of Jesus Christ as reported in the Bible raised Lazarus from the dead. It was not the vigil of his relatives and friends that brought Lazarus back to life. It was divine intervention, according to the story.

In another Biblical story, Daniel faced the lions. His faith in God strengthened him and kept the lions from devouring him. Did Daniel's desire to live have any impact on the outcome?

The serpent who seduced Eve into eating the apple was condemned to spend its life eating earth. Eve's destiny also was altered. She took responsibility for her choice of behavior that was different from what God had advised.

I believe Bible stories can be heard as stepping stones, not as obstacles, in our path to keeping the minds and bodies we have received from God as healthy as possible.

Those stories are sometimes used by Fatalists to support their negative behavior. They do not want to be responsible for being well. Fighters, conversely, are not put off from their sense of responsibility by a tradition of religious helplessness.

Why would a loving God want to punish His creations by making them suffer? Yet sick people often are told, "You don't deserve to suffer like this," as if some people do deserve to suffer. Such statements are not comforting to sick people, since people all have secrets they are ashamed of. You may believe that you deserve being punished for one of them.

There are those who believe they are being held responsible for the negligence of others. Their sickness somehow counterbalances a common pool of punishment for the sins of others.

BLAME

In their efforts to help people change their unwholesome ways of living, some writers seem to blame sick people for the state of their health. Sick people rarely consciously choose to be unhealthy. They are responsible, not guilty. They also deserve compassion and respect.

They are responsible for knowing their family health history. If that history includes a number of relatives who have died early of illnesses stemming from high blood pressure, for example, they are responsible for exercising, eating properly, limiting the use of salt, and avoiding situations of stress.

It is important for them to differentiate between blame and responsibility. Blaming yourself for developing an illness encourages you to use whatever energy you have to ruminate about what you could have done differently. Responsibility allows you to decide what you can do *now* to recover your health.

After my husband suffered a heart attack 16 years ago, I asked one of his cardiologists what I could do to help Bob recover his health. He responded that I shouldn't feel guilty about Bob's attack.

In one of his most endearing moments in our long marriage,

my husband told his doctor that he took full responsibility for his heart attack and did not blame me for any of it.

The physician was accustomed to meeting women who sneaked meatball sandwiches into the intensive care unit or fed their husbands chocolate cake or pizza. The women had guilt feelings because they held themselves responsible for their husbands' health. They did not believe that their husbands were responsible for their own actions. They could refuse items not on their diets. I wasn't feeling guilty. I just wanted to help my husband recover. The doctor, however, did not listen to me but rather dealt with me as a generic wife. I was a stereotype, not an individual, in his eyes.

Individual Fighters are aware of the value of prevention. They are less interested in placing blame and more interested in developing future good health.

ALTERNATIVE HEALERS

Fighters are dedicated to prevention.

They are frequently open to receiving help from alternative sources *as well as* from traditional medical ones. They visit massage therapists, chiropractors, naturopaths, acupuncturists. Some of them accept other sources as a resource—rebirthing sessions, psychic readings, throwing the I Ching.

Yet, what is consistent throughout is that Fighters consider all these sources ancillary to themselves. It is their own "blazing determination," as Norman Cousins said, that will restore them to good health.

Fighters are open to whatever might be of help to them. They do not believe that "there is only one way to skin a cat." Nor do they believe there is only one way to maintain or regain health.

Michael Landon, "Little Joe" in the TV series Bonanza, died of cancer in 1991. Confronted with the side effects of chemotherapy for his terminal illness, Landon chose to use natural substances to eliminate his pain. With their use, he had no more pain, nor did he suffer from hair loss, nausea, or appetite loss. He said (1991), "You can die of the cure before you die of the disease." He was able to concentrate and to have a social life until his death.

Fighters, even in the face of death, make decisions that enhance self-esteem. They do not allow others to decide about their lives.

When a surgeon prescribes surgery for them, they automatically seek a second opinion. If they are told a medical condition they have can't be cured, they seek another doctor. If the doctor they have treats them anonymously, they find another who listens to them and responds to them as a fellow human being, not simply "the cancer in 412."

They are not intimidated by remarks of doctors, friends, or family about "that quack" when they consult an alternative healer. As they widen their search for satisfying health care, they disregard comments about "doctor shopping." They ask traditional doctors for help but see them as consultants, not as the ones who cure. That is a role only they themselves can assume.

Fighters, of course, are not the only ones who seek out such help. A woman who was a skeptical Fatalist told me that what was good about her complicated illness was that it allowed her to visit all kinds of healers around the world for a possible cure. She didn't make any changes in her lifestyle, as befitted a Fatalist. She simply sought out various helpers.

True Fighters are willing to alter their lifestyles in hopes of creating change.

MENTAL IMAGERY AND AFFIRMATIONS

In addition to making use of alternative healers, Fighters use their own minds to help them create a milieu for good health. Some of them practice mental imagery, designing pictures of health. Just as the mind creates pictures when you dream, it also can create pictures when you are awake. Those pictures influence your behavior.

For instance, if you see yourself as robust and vibrant, you do not act as if you are fragile and meek. Wherever you are at this moment, pull your ribcage up and shake your head vigorously. Notice how different you feel, how much more powerful.

To solve difficulties I was having with one of the members on my dissertation committee, I spoke to her by telephone in front of a mirror. As soon as I began to slump or hang my head, I assumed my "diva" pose, that is, I stood or sat up straight and spoke from my diaphragm.

Another method Fighters often use to be healthy is to say "affirmations" to themselves. They are what you say when you talk to yourself.

If what you say to yourself are things like, "You're such a klutz," "What can you expect?," "It's just one more thing," you need to change the sayings into ones that further your cause. When you are feeling very tired, it is useful to say, "I am a fountain of energy." When you are surrounded by people with colds, you might say, "I am in perfect health."

Instead, people often tell themselves foreboding statements like, "I'll probably get sick too." Fighters don't do that. They make their odds more favorable by lessening the mental burden they must overcome to live lives of zest and health.

AGAINST ALL ODDS

A Fighter who granted me an interview is Jane Davidson, whose vision is failing. Jane believes illness runs in her family. Her brother's vision is also failing. Her father and grandfather suffered from poor vision, as well.

Jane's hearing has also diminished. For that she wears a hearing aid.

She tells me, "It was only when I did a workshop with you on family illness that I learned that poor sight and hearing are health problems. You had us do a Life Drawing and I saw that these are weak areas in my family.

"My mother always told me that if I tried harder, I could see or hear. She knew I was dyslexic, but never told me because she thought I'd give up trying. Instead, I thought I was stupid.

"After I had a baby and couldn't hear her cry, I got a hearing aid. My mother told me I was pampering myself."

Because of the lack of family support, Jane surrounds herself with supportive friends. They encourage her to fight the losses she is undergoing.

She follows a physical regimen of good health habits. She doesn't drink or smoke and eats a nutritious diet, and walks several miles a day.

Her parents lived a moderate lifestyle, as well. However, her father, a robust man, was killed by an auto when he was 50 because he did not see the car advancing towards the crosswalk. Her grandfather, a physician, gave up his medical practice because of failing vision.

The family illness, as Jane describes it, is that the Davidsons suffer from not being able to have a good time. Understandably, they are constantly worried about health. When things are going well, they talk about what might go wrong. Jane believes that loss of vision and hearing can be dealt with. But the failure to accept life's joys and sorrows causes depression and moroseness. Jane is determined this will never happen to her.

CHILDHOOD MEMORIES

Another fighter who refuses to accept the family legacy is Norman Winters, a former client of mine. Norman is vice-president of a Fortune 500 corporation. He is accustomed to attending social events peopled with strangers. One of his assets is the ease with which he can converse with them. A frequent comment about him is, "He always makes you feel like he is truly interested in you."

At family gatherings, however, Norman often looks and acts like a young boy. His Aunt May invariably makes comments about her nephew's childhood. She particularly enjoys telling how he screamed when his mother put his security blanket in the wash.

Obviously happy to note the resemblances between her

deceased brother and her nephew, his son, Aunt May frequently says to Norman, "Hearing you speak reminds me so much of my brother." Her eyes well up with tears as she hugs her nephew.

Those comments make the businessman feel awkward, but pleased that someone still sees him as a little boy.

If questions are raised about his health, particularly his blood pressure, Norman grows uncomfortable. Reminders of his father's death at 48 of a stroke make him apprehensive. While resemblances to his father's voice, height, or bearing cause him no trouble, references to possible shared weaknesses fill Norman with dread. He does not want to resemble his father in terms of health.

To avoid receiving such a legacy, Norman jogs, has given up smoking, has lost weight, avoids the use of salt, and meditates. He is a Fighter who doesn't passively accept the family legacy for poor health and an early grave.

STAGE FRIGHT

Unlike Norman Winters who finds it so easy to speak, Paul Rutledge, another client, was at a conference in a foreign country and felt the family legacy surfacing when he began to develop laryngitis that resulted in speechlessness.

Paul's father, a brilliant attorney, frequently developed laryngitis before an especially stressful court hearing and had to ask a colleague to deliver his opening remarks.

Paul knew that his father's behavior was part of his own heritage and decided he wanted no part of it.

"I am not my father. My voice is strong and powerful," he kept saying to himself.

As a child, Paul remembered hearing his father's guffaw floating across the backyard when he played with him and his brothers. Paul delighted in the times when his father threw him up in the air and caught him.

He also remembered the comforting, clucking noises his mother made when her husband, Paul's father, whispered to her that he couldn't speak any louder before a big court case he had been preparing. She encouraged her husband to be well.

Paul spoke to himself encouragingly and repeated the above affirmation about his voice. Paul's voice was again loud and he was ready to give a workshop when it was time for his presentation.

ANNIVERSARY PHENOMENON

Mark Anderson, a believer in having fun, suddenly became impotent as his 40th birthday approached. Seeking help for his sexual problem, Mark visited my office. One of the initial tasks I gave him was to draw up a genogram. After completing the task, Mark shared his feelings about his father's death at 40.

The story emerged that Mark's father had died while having sex with a woman other than his wife. His health history included abuse of his body. He was a heavy smoker and drinker. He was overweight. He rarely exercised. He dealt with stress by gambling.

In none of these ways was Mark like his father. Like him, however, he also avoided delving into emotional issues. (It was only because of the sex problems that Mark agreed to seek help.) He had never expressed his outrage at his father's actions to his father because he was afraid of being physically beaten if he ever spoke out to him. After his father's death, Mark believed there was no point in expressing his anger. And so, he repressed his feelings.

As he approached the age at which his father died, Mark was faced with the remnants of his suppressed feelings for him. Mark was a very shy man, so I assigned him to talk into a tape recorder for one hour as he sat alone in his car. On tape, he was to tell his father all the things he had never told him. Our appointment was scheduled for the hour immediately following this assignment.

When Mark arrived, he was obviously exhausted. His 6'5'' body was wracked by sobs for the first 15 minutes. Then Mark related how he had raged at his father during the first half hour of taping for the times he refused to take him fishing, for the balls he never caught with him, for the times he never tousled his hair, for the hugs he longed for, and finally for humiliating his mother. After Mark raged, he was overcome by profound sadness. Once the anger was removed, he was able to feel empathy for his father, who was a lonely figure, given to various substitute ways of expressing his feelings.

Mark recognized similar traits in himself. He expressed his feelings of love towards his wife solely through sex. When he was impotent, he didn't know how to express his feelings of intimacy with her. He was willing to learn new ways and was hopeful the sexual problem was temporary. (It was.)

Mark changed other parts of his inherited lifestyle as well. He returned to exercising vigorously. He had never had a drinking or gambling problem and didn't smoke. The diet he followed, together with the exercise, quickly led to a leaner, firmer, body.

The biggest change Mark made was in his relationships with his children. He began to spend separate time with each of the three youngsters. Instead of being an unapproachable father, he became someone his children enjoyed talking with. They went fishing together, played "catch," and gave each other hugs.

Mark was determined to teach his children a lifestyle his father had not taught him. A lifestyle of fitness in both mind and body.

Another model he presented his children was to develop a closer relationship with his wife, his mother, and his two younger brothers.

"I want them to see me being intimate with my family. I never saw that."

Another example of the anniversary phenomenon was told me by a couple I was seeing who had marital problems.

Melanie was worried that Ben followed a reckless lifestyle. For example, he refused to buckle his seatbelt, to stop smoking, to lose weight. He liked to fly, climb cliffs, and scuba dive.

When examining their genogram, I noted that the men on *both* sides of the family, including Melanie's first husband, had died at 43. Because of that fact, Melanie was afraid Ben would also die at the fateful age. She wanted him to spend more time with her and their children. He experienced this as pressure, not love.

She was anxious to have him outlive the fateful age for two reasons. One was that she wanted to live the rest of her life with him. The other was that living long, he could leave a legacy of a healthy old age to their children.

A Fatalist, Ben felt that he wanted to live life as zestfully as possible because with the male legacy of his own family, he was destined to die young. After all, his father, grandfather and great-grandfather had all died at 43.

By discussing Melanie's worries and Ben's fatalistic denial of early death, the couple began to understand their deep-seated fears of the power of the anniversary phenomenon.

DEATH OF PARENTS

At the same time as I saw Mark and Ben, I had the opportunity to work with two other men who had problems of impotence. While neither of them was approaching 40, both had had strained relationships with their fathers. They had failed to become close while their fathers were alive.

In each case, an event reminding them of their father's lack of regard for them had triggered the impotence. Clifford Wyeth had become impotent after his wife's mother died. Seeing his wife and her siblings grieve freely provided Clifford with a vision he had never had, of children feeling deeply for their parents. He lamented that he had been unable to express those feelings when his own parents had died. While he held in his feelings, he also became impotent. Expressing his feelings more openly led to his regaining his sexual potency.

The other client, Tom Randolph, became impotent after his father's death. Tom had never been close to him and after he died, Tom failed to grieve for the things that would never be. However, he did release the other feelings he had—his disappointment and anger. After he dealt with these, Tom's sexual performance returned.

Bodies are barometers of what is going on in a person's life. You must respect its signals to you as you would respect storm warnings that the Weather Service provides. The sexual manifestations of the body are as indicative of emotions as are headaches, cancers, heart diseases, or other maladies.

ANTICIPATING A RECURRENT EVENT

When a family expects an event to occur, be it cancer, heart disease or frequent colds, they are not surprised at its appearance. Some families attempt to avoid these occurrences by extraordinary means. They may have healthy breasts removed, what are called prophylactic mastectomies or have both ovaries removed (oopharectomy) or have a prophylactic hysterectomy performed.

While it may seem unbelievable to readers that healthy organs may be removed, it is in fact a reality that they are.

Members of so-called "cancer families" have assented to such surgery after seeing other family members suffer from the disease. It is important that they remain aware of the latest research which provides genetic screening for some cancers.

The fear inherited from one's family about the inevitability of a family illness can have a profound impact on health decisions.

A FEARFUL MOTHER

Ruthie Stankiewicz, a sexually attractive client, was about to undergo elective surgery to "strip" her varicose veins. She called her mother in another state to ask her to stay with her children for the two days she was to be in the hospital. Her mother shrieked that Ruthie could not possibly have surgery. "Don't you realize that you are 34, the fatal age in our family?" Ruthie had no luck trying to reassure her mother, who was certain Ruthie would die if she had surgery. After all, hadn't Ruthie's first cousin died from a cut that caused blood poisoning? "Struck down in the prime of his life. And what about poor Uncle Stanley? And your grandfather?" Then her mother recounted some more gruesome stories about 34-year-olds who had died in the family.

Ruthie loved to swim and had her own pool. A beautiful woman, she was becoming more and more self-conscious about her varicose viens. She wanted surgery to eliminate them. She sought therapy in order to get help in reassuring her mother that Ruthie would be all right.

Ruthie was aware that her family used illness as a way to avoid confrontation. A sick person in the Stankiewicz family was excused from working out problems. Ruthie believed she no longer reverted to that behavior.

Ruthie's mother attended a therapy session to resolve this issue. She was a handsome, vital woman who obviously loved her daughter and grandchildren. In little ways, she displayed her love for them—she brushed a hair from Ruthie's shoulder and later she showed me photos of her grandchildren.

She was very upset that her children had received a legacy of early deaths from her family. She felt guilty about this legacy. Ruthie assured her mother she did not hold her responsible for the family. She trusted her doctor's tests that indicated she was in no risk and she had faith in her own good health. She thanked her mother for her love and concern and absolved her of any responsibility for the surgery.

A week later, Ruthie underwent surgery with no negative aftereffects.

Like other Fighters, Ruthie had a goal and worked towards it.

REMEMBRANCE

Judy Ferguson was recommended to me by her neurologist after a series of tests showed no neurological reason for the migraine headaches she was experiencing.

Judy told me she was prone to getting these headaches each year when the weather turned colder. She assumed the weather or the children returning to school and leaving the house quieter had an impact on the state of her health. However, when a trip to visit her mother in the Caribbean one October where the weather was very different from her home-town did not create any change in her headaches, one of these two possibilities was eliminated. As for the other, there was no way to check it out.

Instead, I had Judy draw a genogram. When she arrived at the birth and death dates of her maternal grandparents, Judy said they died on the same October day in a flu epidemic. A number of Judy's relatives died at the same time.

The event had been glossed over by Judy's mother, but Judy remembered that her mother always checked to see if she had enough clothes on or was cold. Judy did not recall any other specific aftermath of her grandparents' demise.

Somehow I felt there was more to the story. It was too "pat." So again, Judy visited her mother.

Armed with a tape recorder and a story about a sociology class investigating students' roots, Judy asked her mother to recount the story of her parents' death.

"I remember the day they fell ill. My mother's hand seemed on fire when I held it. There was much confusion and arguing. Probably someone was saying the doctor couldn't come. Both my mother and father died that night. I was only eight years old."

Esther, Judy's mother, then began to sob uncontrollably and to speak in Yiddish, the language of her childhood. Judy held her mother to comfort her. Esther soon stopped crying and said the horror was afterwards.

"Thousands of people were dying of the flu. There was no time to have a proper funeral. The next day my uncles took me to the cemetery."

Esther could barely get the words out. Judy gave her a tall glass of iced tea and her mother continued.

"All I remember are rows and rows of coffins piled on top of one another. My mother's brothers kept reading the names and finally found my mother's coffin. They dumped the ones above her onto the path and opened her coffin. They insisted I look in at my mother and kiss her good-bye. She was cold and turning black.

"My uncles yanked her wedding ring off her finger and slammed down the lid.

"I never did see my father's body."

Judy's mother told her how the relatives had moved her from her own house to live with one of her relatives. No one let her mourn her loss. Instead she relived the trauma of the coffins over and over again.

"I'll never forget that day. It was a cold blustery day in October."

Judy now recollected how cranky her mother was each autumn. She would scold Judy and her sister for behavior that was disregarded at other times of the year.

Esther and her husband had their loudest fights each year in the Fall.

Now Judy understood why her own anxiety increased each year in October. She had made a negative connection with that time of year. After reaching this understanding, Judy no longer suffered headaches. And she no longer had bouts of anxiety from unknown sources.

Judy believed that the anniversary phenomenon was programmed to exist for later generations if not brought to light by her. And so, to put an end to its continuance, Judy played the tape for her children and described the impact these events had had on her mother and herself.

Awareness that you are following a program laid out by someone else's experiences frees you to live a life of your own design. You are not destined by biology to live someone else's life.

CHRONIC ILLNESS

Annabelle Pagano had grown up watching her mother's health progressively deteriorate as a result of multiple sclerosis (MS). This is an illness that often shows up in a number of members of the same family.

At the age of 35, Annabelle began to notice changes in her athletic ability. She no longer had the stamina to spend a day on the ski slopes. When she jogged, one of her feet dropped flatly under her.

Fearing that she was following in her mother's footsteps, Annabelle sought medical help and, after extensive testing, was diagnosed as having MS. At first, she denied it was so and simply coped with it as well as she could. "I called on all my coping skills but none were working."

About the time her illness was diagnosed, Annabelle was separated from her large network of friends because of her husband's job relocation. Talking with friends by telephone, she tended to deny the terror she felt about having the illness.

In her new home, Annabelle had to search for doctors, friends, and a church. Her daughter entered high school and began to disengage from the family. Her husband was involved in establishing himself in a new business setting. Annabelle had much time on her hands and no familiar ways to utilize it. She could not jog, do aerobics, or bicycle.

Eventually, she had to face the fact that she was no longer able to move about without help of some sort—a cane, banisters— and that her energy level was very low. It was then that she began lessons in biofeedback and learned to produce 10-minute trances rather than take long naps. "I slipped into a spiritual mode." By this she meant that periods of meditation became a part of each day.

Meditation caused Annabelle to recognize that she had been expressing much anger toward her husband and daughter over trivial issues. She realized that expressing her anger at having the illness was more frightening to her than showing anger toward the two people who loved her most of all, her husband and her daughter. Being angry with them allowed her to ventilate her emotions.

It was not until she felt more in control of those emotions that Annabelle disclosed to her mother that she too had MS. Her mother advised her how to accept the illness, not how to fight it.

Annabelle enrolled in a graduate program in economics. She plans to work with the poor. She practices yoga daily so that her muscles remain as firm as possible. She performs deep breathing exercises so that her breathing is at a peak level.

Annabelle was unwilling to be like her mother and wait for more and more disability to enter her life. She felt her mother had made a career of MS. She refuses to live the helpless model she sees in her mother.

Fighters empower themselves. They do not passively accept other people's picture of their future. Fighters create their own picture even including how to deal with chronic illness.

GOALS

Fighters always have goals. When you ask them what they look forward to, they give you specific answers. Not for them vague answers like, "We'll see" or "Something will come up."

To set goals, they have a vision of the future. The picture is an inclusive one. They don't look at it from afar, but are a major part of it.

To help you in creating that picture, you can make a collage of yourself.

Collect a pile of magazines. Any kind will do—news weeklies, scandal magazines, housekeeping monthlies, travel tabloids.

Give yourself 10 minutes to scan the contents for pictures that you want in your life. You may pick ones that convey a relaxed life on a sunny beach, one of a skier careening down a mountain of snow, a child running on a city street. Whatever photos you pick, let them have some meaning to you. Cut them out.

Then cut out any words that describe you, as you are or as you hope to be—"Sexy," "CEO," "Great Cook," "Healthy," "Fun."

Glue the pictures onto a piece of posterboard. You are making a poster of you.

When it is finished, you can ask yourself some questions: "Who am I?" "How do I want to present myself to others?" "Do I like the pictures I've made?" "Are there significant gaps in my pictures?" "What is edited out?"

Your next project is to write three health goals on separate index cards—one for each goal.

Having specific goals for maintaining or developing good health is necessary to reaching your goal. For a person with severe arthritis, a goal may be spending two hours without pain; one of the goals for someone with lupus may be to have the energy to write letters; someone with heart disease may work towards being able to have sex without taking a nitroglycerin pill.

Good health goals require facing up to the limitations you have. One 50-year-old man who had had two heart attacks 10 years previously defined his goal of good health as "being the way I was before the heart attacks." However, no amount of work was going to replace his scarred heart with an unscarred one.

Setting goals with one overweight client was very difficult. "Deciding to eat sensibly for the rest of my life is scary."

Fighters can go to a banquet with friends and avoid those foods that are not good for them.

Fighters have firm commitments to themselves. For example, they might walk four miles three days a week. They swim at the "Y" every morning before work. They always park at the farthest spot at the mall so they are forced to walk as far as possible. They ski twice a week in cold weather and play tennis twice a week the year round. Fighters automatically do the things that will keep them well. They do not have to decide each day whether or not they will take charge of their health.

THE COST OF ILLNESS

Fighters who practice wellness techniques should not have to assume medical and insurance costs of those who don't. The high cost of health insurance is predicated on those who use insurance most often. Smokers, for example, cause the insurance rate for nonsmokers to be higher than it would be without smokers in the pool of insured persons.

General Motors discovered the costs of their cars were

inflated because the cost of insurance for their workers was so high. They began to provide gyms and healthier foods on-site. They demonstrated to their workers their support of prevention.

The corporate giant did not blame its workers for sickness. Instead, it supported workers' responsibility for good health. The company made it easy to use the gym and to obtain foods that are better for health.

It has not yet become common for the culture to support efforts of Fighters to maintain good health. Hopefully, the term Fighters will be obsolete after their efforts to be well become the usual actions in our society.

ACTIVITIES

1. Think over the last six months. How have you responded to challenges? What did you do? For instance, what measures did you take after losing a special account? How did you resolve an argument with a friend?
2. Design a picture of yourself in three months, six months, and one year. What will you do to develop those pictures?
3. If you are a Fighter on some issues, why not on others? Are you influenced by the expectations of your boss? Do you feel you don't want to let the team down? Do you join groups that share common purposes with you?

6

FATALIST OR FIGHTER
Which Will You Be?

Betty Haskins' family was not surprised when she told them she had breast cancer. Breast cancer was common among her women relatives.

At first, Betty accepted her diagnosis. She visited her lawyer to make out a new will and set special treasures aside for favorite friends or relatives.

It was only when she read a magazine article about a woman with a history similar to her own who had decided to fight her way back to good health that Betty decided to disinherit herself of the family legacy.

She closed her boutique and went to Santa Fe. There she met others who had taken charge of their own destinies.

They advised her to find out what her body was telling her needed to be done. To hear her body, Betty began to meditate twice a day.

Calming her mind, through meditation, allowed Betty to be in touch with her body. She learned she was saddened by her emotional distance from her sister and physical distance from her two grown daughters.

Betty realized she had to take a more active role in reestablishing family connections. She began to write notes and call her family members. She arranged a visit to Norway where her grandfather had lived before emigrating to America. Many of her relatives still lived there.

She began to find health practitioners who were willing to listen to her. Her bodily healing began to occur.

Betty's fatalistic attitude evolved into one of taking command of her life. She became a Fighter.

THE FATALIST IN YOU

Since you are reading this book, you probably have some serious concerns about illness that runs in your family. You may wonder if you are doomed to inherit it. Are you a Fatalist?

Do you believe that:

- you have no control over your present and future health?
- the time of your death is predetermined?
- you will have a short or long life because your parents did?
- adopting a healthy diet and sensible exercise regimen to preserve your health is not worth the trouble?
- altering particular habits will not improve your general health?

Do you agree with these sayings?

- Live fast, die young, and make a handsome corpse.
- Eat, drink and be merry for tomorrow we die.
- When your number's up, it's up.
- Life is a crap game—all luck.

Do you often say things like these?

- This isn't my day.
- That's the way the cookie crumbles.
- Just hanging in.
- It's just my luck.

If you are a Fatalist, you probably answered yes to many of these questions.

THE FIGHTER IN YOU

To determine if you are a Fighter, the following questions will help.

Do you believe that . . .

- you can change anything if you put your mind to it?
- you are not at the mercy of chance?
- just because your parents did, you don't have to die young?
- living a healthy life is worth the effort?

Do you agree with these sayings?

- Anything is possible.
- Don't cry over spilled milk.
- When the going gets tough, the tough get going.
- Never hope more than you work.

Do you often say things like these?

- Let me work at it a little more.
- I can't believe my luck.
- Everything's coming up roses.

Fighters will answer yes to most of these questions.

Both Fatalists and Fighters must decide if there is any point to having good health. What would they do with the added energy? Would they have a stronger sex drive? Would they work harder in the garden? Would they write the book they have always wanted to?

What would life be like without the fear of illness? The following Health Assessment will let you know.

HEALTH ASSESSMENT

I. Personal choices	Always	Some- times	Never
1. Do you visit the dentist at least once a year?	☑	☐	☐
2. Do you use dental floss daily?	☐	☑	☐
3. Do you have your vision checked regularly?	☐	☑	☐
4. Do you question your doctor about the necessity of the drugs he/she prescribes for you when you're ill?	☐	☑	☐
5. Are you reluctant to use laxatives, tranquilizers, painkillers, reducing pills, and aspirin?	☐	☑	☐
6. Have you ever asked your doctor for a nonmedical alternative?	☐	☐	☑
7. Have you ever disregarded the doctor's advice completely?	☐	☐	☑
8. Do you have health insurance?	☑	☐	☐
9. Do you wear a seat belt while riding in or driving a car?	☑	☐	☐
10. Would you willingly visit a psychotherapist if it seemed indicated?	☑	☐	☐
11. Do you keep a health journal?	☐	☐	☑

II. Body Awareness	Always	Some- times	Never
1. Do you have satisfactory sexual relationships?	☐	☑	☐
2. Are you pleased with the quality of your sexual relationships?	☐	☑	☐

3. Do you practice yoga or some form of stretching exercise at least 20 minutes three times or more a week? □ ☑ □
4. Do you jog or participate in some type of exercise at least three times a week? □ ☑ □
5. Do you fall asleep easily at bedtime? ☑ □ □
6. Do you feel rested when you awaken? □ ☑ □
7. Is your weight within five percent of the ideal for your height? □ ☑ □
8. Do you have enough energy to accomplish your daily activities? □ ☑ □
9. Do you feel at ease with your body? □ ☑ □
10. Do you breathe deeply and fully? □ ☑ □
11. Do you see an illness as an indication that something is out of balance in your lifestyle? ☑ □ □
12. When you are sick, do you find it easy to stop work, relax and rest? ☑ □ □
13. Do you refuse to smoke cigarettes? □ ☑ □

III. STRESS AND STRESS MANAGEMET

1. Do you engage in any creative activities either alone or with a group? □ ☑ □
2. Do you feel it is O.K. to get angry or say "No" to someone? ☑ □ □
3. Are you able to resolve conflict when it occurs? ☑ □ □

4. Are you able to recognize when worry and anxiety increase to the point of interfering with your lifestyle? ☑ ☐ ☐

5. Do you feel that the best way to deal with strong emotional feelings is to confront them? ☑ ☐ ☐

6. Do you regularly reduce stress by setting aside a time for yourself to use a specific relaxation technique? ☐ ☑ ☐

7. Do you use massage or some other type of "hands on" method for relaxation? ☐ ☑ ☐

8. Do you set aside at least one hour each day for "play," that is, some activity that is done for enjoyment only? ☐ ☑ ☐

IV. ENVIRONMENTAL AWARENESS

1. Do you make use of transportation other than automobiles when possible? ☑ ☐ ☐

2. Do you keep your thermostat at 65 or lower in the winter? ☐ ☐ ☑

3. Do you use nonpolluting and nontoxic cleaning agents and avoid exposure to chemicals, sprays, and exhaust fumes? ☐ ☑ ☐

V. NUTRITIONAL AWARENESS

1. Do you eat your meals in a quiet relaxed environment? ☐ ☑ ☐

2. Do you eat at least one uncooked fruit or vegetable per day? ☐ ☑ ☐

3. Do you limit the use of coffee and nonherbal teas to three cups per day? ☑ ☐ ☐

4. Do you read labels carefully to check for food additives? □ ☑ □

5. Do you eat well-balanced meals selected from the four basic food groups? □ ☑ □

6. Are you aware of your own nutritional needs and how to meet them? □ ☑ □

7. Do you limit the consumption of alcohol to minimal amounts? ☑ □ □

14 24 4

After finishing this inventory, tally the items you have checked under "Never," "Sometimes," and "Always."

If your "Never" score adds up to over 10, it is likely that you feel at the mercy of life events. You are a Fatalist about your health.

If your "Never" score is under 3, you are a Fighter. Being told there is nothing you can do about a legacy of poor health and early death doesn't put you into a tailspin. You don't believe it.

A score of 10 or more "Sometimes" indicates you are a skeptical Fatalist. You waver about believing you have power over your life. Eating an apple at lunchtime is like carrying a rabbit's foot for you. It might have some magic, so there is no harm in it.

A score of 30 or more "Always" is a good indicator that you are a Fighter. You take responsibility for good health.

You can strengthen your beliefs in your personal power if they are low. Read on.

1. Are there any areas you feel you would like to change? Can you eat a better diet, fasten your seatbelt, floss your teeth? In what specific ways do you commit yourself to a self-regimen of care and reverence in the future? List them below.

Exercise more

2. From what you wrote above, circle the three goals most important to you. What do you most want to accomplish?

3. How will you specifically attain each goal? Write out your plan. What will you do first? Second?

4. Set a deadline for each new behavior. Be realistic. It is not feasible for you to change a series of lifelong habits overnight.

5. How will you celebrate your achievements? If you'd like to take a balloon flight, promise yourself that. Maybe you want to have a party for 20 people celebrating your courage to change.

If you want to assess your answers individually, turn to Appendix I in the back of the book.

YOU AS YOUR OWN HEALTH BAROMETER

Dr. John Bailer, an epidemiologist at McGill University in Montreal, says, "It's ludicrous to find people worried about this kind of exposure (electric blankets, sunlight, Xrays, health hazards) while they continue to smoke, continue to eat a rotten diet, or drive around without seat belts."

Once we have determined to change some specific health habits, we must be optimistic about our efforts. Unlike Beth James, whom we met in Chapter 4, we have to believe our new habits will be effective. An "It won't make any difference" attitude will hardly spur us on to defeat inertia and the natural reluctance to perform difficult, sometimes boring, but consistent new health habits.

Fatalists are easy prey to despair. Because they believe that outside authorities know more about them than they do, they easily give up former good health habits when told they have a fatal illness. Fighters accept the diagnosis with respect, but know they are the final arbiter on themselves. Not only do they continue to practice healthy habits, but they are certain they will recover or maintain good health.

Being loyal to one's family may mean developing an illness that repeats itself among your forebears. Not developing that illness is a kind of disloyalty to your family and requires much courage.

A certain amount of courage is required to refuse the family legacy of poor health. Family tradition is very powerful, even if the tradition is that of developing illness. You can create a new tradition for yourself.

A FUTURE PLAN

It is possible to teach "old dogs new tricks." Of course, it is better to have been taught correctly from the beginning. If you have not been taught correctly, all is not lost, however. You can design a healthy future.

You must schedule your time so that you learn new habits. Fatalists say, "I have no time." Fighters make time.

A retired client in her 70s was told she had high blood pressure, like other members of her family. She determined to use natural means to bring her blood pressure down. She decided to learn to swim. Three mornings a week she visited the local YMCA for swimming lessons.

"I always regretted that my parents had not taught me to swim. I decided I could give myself permission to learn."

Now Mildred swims every day to keep her blood pressure regulated. She makes time for her body to be well. Mildred is a Fighter.

Fighters won't accept a modular plan—one that would suit anyone. It must be individually crafted for them and the only architects can be themselves. No one else knows what will suit them.

DIFFERENCES IN PREPARING FOR PHYSICIAN VISITS

First of all, Fighters prepare for a visit to a health-care practitioner.

They do so by delineating the goals they wish to reach as a result of attending the appointment. They make sure their goals are precise. They ask themselves what they want to know.

If tests have been advised, they ask why. "What will tests show? Where will they be performed, at the doctor's office or a hospital laboratory?" They want to know how to prepare for the test.

And finally, they want to know what they can expect next.

Often, Fatalists don't ask their doctors questions that give them information. But Fighters are curious and ask.

NO MEDICATION

Fighters such as Mildred prefer to learn self-help methods that will return them to good health or keep them there by non-medical means. They are often unwilling to take medication for ailments. When they visit a physician's office, it is to learn how they can help themselves rather than what the physician can do to cure them.

Regardless, the doctor almost automatically writes out a prescription for some medication.

At that point, the Fatalist merely takes the form. However, before the physician can exit the room, the Fighter asks questions.

"What is this for?"
"How long will I need to take it?"
"How will you assess if it has been effective?"
"What does it cost?"
"Is there a substitute that is less expensive?"
"What can I do besides taking this medication?"
"What did they do in the old days before this medication?"

RESPONSE ASSESSMENT

To determine what you challenge and what you don't and to better establish if you are a Fatalist or a Fighter, complete the following short series of questions:

1. When you see a truck heading straight towards you on the highway . . .
    A. Do you say "Oh, shit" and wait for impact?
    B. Do you try to veer off the road as far as possible?
    C. Do you put your arm out to protect your unseat-belted spouse?
2. At your annual dental checkup . . .
    A. Do you await the bad news?
    B. Do you request watching a video on the proper techniques for brushing and flossing?
    C. Does the dentist find many problems that could have been avoided through better care?
3. When you're in a rush at lunchtime, do you . . .
    A. Get a hamburger and fries at the nearest fast food restaurant?
    B. Take a walk around the block?
    C. Get a yogurt and a piece of fruit?
4. When you shop for a new outfit to wear to your class reunion and your usual size is too small, do you . . .

    A. Go on a diet that uses special foods?

    B. Decide not to go to the reunion?

    C. Immediately eliminate all the "extras" from your diet?

5. In a traffic jam, do you . . .

    A. Leave the road you're on to explore a new road?

    B. Fume about getting to work on time?

    C. Turn to relaxing music on the radio or put a talking book on the tape deck?

6. When there is a forecast, of a possible tornado, do you . . .

    A. Open the windows so the wind won't blow them out?

    B. Call everyone you know who might be affected to warn them?

    C. Figure the tornado will blow everything of value away?

Your answers to these questions will help you analyze the general trend you have to feel powerless or to consider options.

In question 1, did you choose A, B, or C? A is the sign of a Fatalist. B is a Fighter's choice. C is a Fatalist who doesn't plan for the future, but in the crunch tries to do something to offset his or her negligence.

For Question 2, A is the sign of a Fatalist. B shows future goals and is a sign of a Fighter. C reenforces the experiences of a Fatalist.

Question 3 has Fatalists again picking A. Fighters choose B or C.

In Question 4, Fatalists are likely to choose A, the last minute answer. And even B shows a feeling of powerlessness. Fighters choose C if they are overweight. That is an experience they rarely know.

For Question 5, Fighters choose A or C. Fatalists seldom consider their options. They would choose B.

In the final question, Fighters might call their friends and warn them of the possibility, Choice B. They might prepare for the worst, Choice A. But Fatalists do not believe any preparation would be effective. They choose C.

HOW TO CHANGE

Dr. Christopher Peterson at the University of Michigan says it is possible to change oneself from a Fatalist to a Fighter. These are the points he made in a meeting of the National Institute for the Clinical Application of Behavioral Medicine in Orlando, Florida in December of 1991:

1. *Use skills in one area to help in another area.* If you are good at scheduling yourself to brush your teeth, for example, use that same strategy to practice stress management. Rather than *promising* to meditate for an hour each morning and middle evening, meditate for five minutes before each meal.
2. *Get into volunteer work.* Volunteering for two hours a day on your way home from work may be better for you than scheduling one day a week.
3. *Work with children.* Whatever age children are fun for you, work with that age.
4. *Set reachable goals.* Instead of wanting to be fifty pounds lighter, plan on losing a half pound a week.
5. *Get a support system to help you achieve your goals.* A support system may be a group at your church, synagogue or temple. It may be a group of friends or relatives. It may be a group run by your local hospital.

   It is important to share your needs with others. Dr. David Spiegel at Stanford found that women recovering from metastatic breast cancer did better when they were part of a support group.
6. *Do things. This feeds back into optimism.* What you do is not as important as that you actually do it. It may be taking a class at the Adult School in your community. Or planning a garden that attracts butterflies.

I have a sign in my waiting room that reads IF YOU ALWAYS DO WHAT YOU'VE ALWAYS DONE, THEN YOU'LL ALWAYS GET WHAT YOU'VE ALWAYS GOTTEN.

Fatalists do the same thing over and over; Fighters are interested in developing new options. If you are reading this book willingly, you probably don't need to discover if you are a Fatalist or a Fighter. You are a Fighter.

ACTIVITIES

1. When are you more vulnerable to giving up trying and giving in to inertia?
2. How do you sabotage yourself?
3. When you are feeling ill, whom do you surround yourself with?
4. How do you replenish your energy?

7

YOU AND THE HEALTH CARE PRACTITIONER

Tom Lubeck did not feel well. He had been suffering from a feeling of nausea after each meal. Instead of his usual enjoyment of food, he had taken to being mildly apprehensive about how he would feel after he ate.

Today was no different. He ordered lunch at The Golden Bowl with much care. A salad with oil and vinegar, a turkey sandwich without mayonnaise, and a frozen yogurt to top it off. He ordered herbal tea to accompany the meal.

Later in the day, he planned to meet with the third physician he had consulted about his malaise. This doctor had been recommended by a colleague of Tom's, also an accountant.

Because Tom had been disappointed with the other doctors' summations that "It isn't time to change your will" and "All is well," he had pursued his quest to find a satisfactory physician. He had a plan to attain his goal.

First, Tom had obtained records of all the tests performed at the other doctors' requests. He had compiled his own file of test results, medications taken, side effects of each drug. He had found that valuable time is lost obtaining such records from each doctor for the next doctor who wants that information. Tom had made a copy of his file for the new doctor.

He had also written out what he wanted to know:

"What is your hunch about why I have these symptoms?"
"How do you plan to go about discovering if your hunch is
    correct? Tests, exams, consultations?"
"What treatment plan will you suggest if I have what you
    suspect?"
"How soon will you know if the treatment is working?"
"How often will I need to see you?"
"How will you ascertain if positive change is occurring?"

Tom's secretary had typed up her boss' questions and left
space after each where Tom could write down the answers as the
doctor gave them to him.

Unlike most people who believe that the first physician they
meet is the one whose treatment they must follow, Tom believed
that he would keep looking until he found a health-care practitioner who could solve the mystery about his nausea. Armed
with his questions and the inevitable nausea, Tom set out to
meet the new physician. He hoped the man would hear him.

LISTENING AND HEARING

One of the most important factors in finding a personal physician is ascertaining if that person "hears" you.

How do you do that?

Betty Haskins (whom you met in Chapter 6) did it by first
learning to *listen to herself.* She began to meditate twice a day
so she could hear herself. Others learn to listen to themselves by
noticing their bodily reactions to certain stimuli. Always feeling worse after being with a certain doctor, for example, causes
them to listen to their bodies. Having enough faith to listen to
yourself will allow you to discover if you feel satisfied with the
doctor you are seeing. Can you say with certainty, "I have been
listened to"? Do you have confidence that the health-care practitioner views you as a unique person, not just as another
patient? Did you get to say what was on your mind?

The answer to being heard is not novel. It is first necessary to
hear yourself. What do you want? Betty discovered what she

wanted through meditation. Tom's method was more trial and error. He didn't know what he wanted, but was able to recognize what he didn't want. He didn't want to be put into a category of "difficult patients." He simply wanted an answer to his physical problem.

TOM'S INITIAL VISIT

With his list in his briefcase along with some papers he was working on at the office, he strode briskly to the doctor's office.

What he found was intimidating. First there was a cadre of nurses, dressed in white, ministering to the doctor. (Tom got the impression of a host of angels ministering to a deity.) The chairs were upright and firm. In some of them were patients obviously very ill.

On this, his initial visit, Tom was given a booklet filled with questions to answer. After filling in the blanks requesting name and address, he was asked for the insurance carrier he used and for the account number he holds.

So far there was no hint of caring. But Tom turned the next page with hope. None was forthcoming.

On the next page and those that followed, Tom was asked to check any symptoms experienced. These were divided into Gastro-Intestinal, Heart, Nervous System, Liver and Kidney Function, Skin Disorders. Did he experience frequent headaches? Blurred vision? Stumbling? Failing memory? Was he tired? Did he have chest pains or shortness of breath? What was his frequency of urination? The list asked him to check the illnesses he had as a child—mumps, chicken pox, etc.

After completing the form, Tom returned it to the nurses. One of them weighed him and took his blood pressure. He was told the doctor would not be long. He waited, well beyond the appointed time, to see Dr. Jones.

When he finally did see Tom, Dr. Jones scanned his completed information form perfunctorily and asked him what he was there for.

Tom's answers were frequently hurried along by "Uh-huhs"

and a close following question. Studies described by Norman
Cousins in *Omni* (1989) show that physicians on average listen
to patients approximately 10 seconds before interrupting them.
After a few minutes of this, Tom was led into an examining room.

In a short, paper robe, he was palpated, scrutinized, and
probed. The doctor ordered laboratory tests to be performed. He
advised Tom that he could be back in touch with the doctor in
a few days to receive the results. (However, if a Pap smear or
mammogram are performed, you are often told that you will not
be called if all is well. It is the "No news is good news"
approach to medicine.) Tom had anticipated the first part of the
initial visit. Now he mobilized his plan. He opened his briefcase and took out his list.

"I have a few items here I would like answered," he began.

The doctor sat back and prepared to listen.

"As you know, I have consulted two other doctors about my
nausea. One checked me for heart trouble, the other for ulcers.
I gave you a copy of their test results for your file.

"What I want to know is what your professional hunch is.
What do you think I have?"

The doctor told him he believed he might have either a sluggish immune system or an allergic response to something he
was eating, or to some vitamins or drugs he was taking, or to a
substance he was using such as dish detergent or laundry soap.
He described the tests required to discover if either was true.

Tom asked what treatment plan would be suggested if the
problem was with his immune system and what it would be if
some allergy was found.

Again the doctor responded readily and also told Tom of possible side effects to the treatment for his immune system.

In looking over his list of questions, Tom saw that half of them
were already answered. He asked the remaining ones: "How often
will I need to see you?" Dr. Jones answered him, "I can't say until
all the test results are in. If it is your immune system, I would
need to see you once a month for three to four months and retest
your blood. If it is an allergy, I will probably see you once more."

"Suppose it is neither of these two possibilities," Tom asked.

"Well then, it's back to the drawing board. But we should

know within two weeks if either of these possibilities is correct."

The entire interview including the shaking of hands took five minutes. In those five minutes, however, Tom felt listened to and his new doctor felt like a caregiver, not like a medical robot.

CARING AND REVERENCE

Caring requires the caregiver to care for and respect the person requesting help. It requires more than love. Love can be given to any fellow being or even to a thing. There was no question that I loved my elderly father, but when I cut his toenails, my love for him was expressed in a caring way. A way he could not mistake.

Reverence requires a willingness to notice what your body is telling you. You must listen to the details, not be impatient with them. You must determine to pay attention to whatever it is your body is expressing. One of my friends develops an itchy left foot when she is out of balance in her life. A man I know, as a child, developed a fiery red ear lobe when his life was out of order. Respecting the body messages rather then taking a pill to relieve symptoms entails a reverence for the fact that the body speaks in symbols, or symptoms, as they are called.

In order to develop caring and reverence, you must learn to listen to the symptoms your body creates for you. You can learn from babies. Babies are fascinated by their body parts. They love to put their feet in their mouths or suck their thumbs.

For an adult to reconnect with body feelings may require planning. Foot or body massage helps. By learning to recognize subtle changes in the body—whether congested toes or rigid neck—you show your body that you care about it. You are not impatient with your organs' physical efforts to signal distress to you.

Heart patients have a history of ignoring symptoms before finally suffering a heart attack. Most of them later admit to having felt tired, experiencing chest pains, especially after exertion, being nauseated frequently. Yet they refused to treat themselves with care and reverence. The signals were ignored. Their bodies eventually expressed "dis-ease" in a more dramatic and visible way—a heart attack.

I advise my clents to treat themselves as "burned babies"—with tenderness—when they have many burdens. Most people treat themselves with impatience, toughness, and practicality when they are undergoing physical or mental distress.

Those lifestyles are learned as children. My mother, a farmer, used to tell my brother, sisters and me, "Don't be such a calf." That meant to her that we shouldn't make a fuss over some simple matter—whether health-related or any other of life's difficulties.

It wasn't until I was writing this book that I spent time watching a cow with its calf. I learned that the calf makes its needs known—the need to be nuzzled, to be licked from head to toe, to be nursed. The calf doesn't give up until help is received. Not a bad lesson to learn.

The persistence and awareness of its needs expressed by a calf are not squelched by other cows saying, "Don't be such a baby," "Big boys don't cry," "You'll get over it." Those dicta can be unlearned by adults. They can say to themselves when something good happens to them, "I deserve it." When something not so good happens they can say, "The child in me needs to be reassured."

As an adult, I tell my family and friends sometimes that I need a good cheerleading talk from them. I am not ashamed to voice my needs. Nor are they. My son's office is in the same building as mine. A few years ago when I was in the throes of writing the dissertation required to complete my doctorate, he commented that I looked like someone who needed a hug. He proceeded to give me one.

When you make external changes but do not change your core beliefs, you are at risk of giving up those changes when you no longer have the support system that encouraged you to make them.

Ted Manzi changed his sedentary behavior by walking five miles and practicing yoga each day. He began to eat a vegetarian diet. He meditated daily. He had fun in his job.

After his support group, a yoga ashram, moved to another

state, Ted lost their encouragement. His internal beliefs had not changed and without his support group, he could not maintain his external actions.

You can design your life so that there are opportunities in it for getting what you need. Even if your life is currently arranged to be unhealthy, you can change it. You can be the *author* of your life, not its editor.

PREVENTION

To author your own life, you must learn what lifestyle is healthy. The National Cancer Society and the American Heart Association provide recommendations for a healthier life. First among their warnings is to stop smoking. Then they recommend diets high in fiber and low in fats. They advise exercise and the use of stress management techniques. They also urge weight loss if a person is overweight.

Rather than constant surveillance and good habits, some people prefer to eliminate the possibility of developing diseased organs by eliminating those organs through prophylactic surgery. The medical rationale for such surgery, as described by researchers at the Sloan-Kettering Hospital in NYC and the U. of Texas Medical School, is that such elimination may decrease the danger of certain site cancers.

Such a theory is analogous to banning cars because there are crashes on highways.

In *Circulation*, the cardiology journal, information was provided demonstrating that those who have had coronary bypass surgery have been shown to need another bypass in five to seven years (Killip, 1985). The findings are that the reasons a heart patient had coronary disease in the first place continued. If a person does not change lifestyle, diet, smoking, weight loss, exercise and stress management, the original problems persist.

Being trim requires attention to diet for most people. Eating moderately demands commitment, especially for persons who have not been careful about their former eating habits. It is very rare that persons have high cholesterol at birth but it does happen. Hyperlipidemia runs in families and no amount of change in diet helps someone who has it. It is a disease that can be detected early and treated.

Persons who are from families in which early deaths of many people occur from the same cause can almost certainly surmise that that disease is hereditary. As much information as possible on prevention of that malady should be obtained. (See Appendix B for a listing of whom to contact for such information.)

Even when one follows the healthiest lifestyle, sometimes sickness occurs. When you first feel sick, you probably treat yourself with remedies learned in your family-of-origin, drinking hot water with lemon and whiskey, for example. If that doesn't work in a few days, the next step may be to consult with your sister, a nurse friend, or a trusted cousin. With their advice and encouragement, the next step may be to set up an appointment with a health-care professional.

PREPARING FOR THE FIRST VISIT

All of these common procedures are good ones to follow. They can be added to the following seven points which should be adopted *before* you visit your practitioner:

1. Listen to yourself. What is bothering you? Unless you know what signals are prompting you to seek medical help, you cannot articulate your needs.
2. Keep a medical log of your daily health. Acute causes to see a doctor are obvious—a broken leg, a bleeding cut above an eye, a sharp, immobilizing chest pain. Chronic lack of sleep, blood in stools, blurred vision usually persist for a while. During that time, it is wise to keep a health journal. When you seek help, you will be more conscious of bodily dysfunction. A health journal should be kept in the same manner you keep a checkbook, with notations of anything out of the ordinary in your health.
3. List the goals you have in seeking help. How will you

know if you get what you want? Write out your goals as Tom Lubeck did. Leave a space to write in whether or not your goals are met. For example, finding out how to lessen your cholesterol level: "I will take home a diet." "My goal was met."

4. Let others know of your health problems. They may know someone who has recovered from the same thing. Ask them whom they saw for help. What treatment did they have? How would they have handled the problem differently if they were to redo it?

5. Research the illness at your library. Most libraries have computers. By typing in "vision," for example, and then adding "blurred," you will find the latest information on that malady. Abstracts of the articles are frequently available on the spot. Articles will be obtained for you. Some libraries do not charge for this service. Others do.

    Some local hospital libraries are open to non-staff. Searches of medical databases can be done there. A Medline Search may cost $10.00 or more. It will give you the most current medical information on your symptoms.

6. Collect all your medical records and films so you will have them on hand for your doctor's information. Having a file of your own saves needless delay when you are consulting another physician. Besides, legally the records are yours and should be in your possession.

7. Check your doctor's policy on confidentiality when you are making the appointment, especially if you are not yet 21. You will want to feel that you can discuss anything and have it kept private.

    After preparing yourself in these ways, you are ready to visit your doctor.

ROLEPLAY

Another way you might want to prepare for a health visit is to roleplay what you will say there. Anne Duffy changed from the physician who planned on performing a hysterectomy as she grew older. Anne roleplayed her final visit to that gynecologist with me.

> "Hello, Dr. Curtis."
> "Hello, Anne. How are you today?"
> "I'm fine. I'm here to receive my annual Pap smear and breast exam. I also want a cervical exam."
> "Yes, it's about time for you to have a hysterectomy."
> "Why do you say that?"
> "Well, all the other women in your family have had them. And you're getting to that age."
> "I don't plan on needing a hysterectomy."
> "We'll see."

Anne had to roleplay about six times before she was ready to visit her gynecologist. It was very hard for her to consider herself an equal to the man she always obeyed in a passive manner.

One of the reasons it is necessary to write out goals and to roleplay your visit before you appear at your doctor's office is that it is difficult to be firm about what you want from a physician, who can appear God-like.

CHANGING THE SCENE

You can change this scenario to one of mature equals who display care and reverence for one another. Let me reiterate how to do this.

The #1 rule is to prepare for the visit as Tom did. Even my car mechanic asks me to compile a list of car maladies before I arrive at the service station. My body deserves at least as much forethought as my car.

The second rule is to delineate the goals you wish to reach as a result of attending the appointment. Make sure your goals are very specific. What do you want to know? A vague discussion about having to expect some difficulties now that you're getting older will not do.

The third step is to write down the answers to your prewritten questions as you receive the answers in the doctor's office. Do not leave the office with any of your questions blank.

If you arrive home with blanks on your sheet, you have a pretty good assessment tool of your communication skills. You will know if you are intimidated by your physician. Are you afraid to ask questions about your own body? After all, without malfunctioning bodies, physicians would be out of business.

If tests have been advised, you need to know why. What will they show? Where will they be performed, at the doctor's office or a hospital laboratory? How should you prepare for the test?

Finally, what can you expect next? If your reason for medical treatment is a straightforward one—a premarital blood test, for example—no further contact may be required.

On the other hand, an annual Pap smear or mammogram may be the occasion to discuss what is right with the test. (I remember one gynecologist telling me my uterus was "as clean as a whistle.")

For more involved procedures, testing for unusual tiredness, for example, a schedule of when you can personally speak to the doctor about the results may be in order. Receiving a comment that "All is well" from a nurse may only raise further questions you want your doctor to answer.

When questions are not answered, consider what information you seek. Do you consult a friend's daughter who is a nurse? Do you listen to stories told you at the office or health club about people with similar symptoms? Those stories and the nurse's explanation may seem more understandable than the information your doctor tells you. If that is the case, it is time to seek out a new doctor.

THE NEW CAREGIVER

Becoming more self-reliant does not mean minimizing the importance of health-care practitioners who can be used as consultants. It means treating them with as much care and reverence as you treat yourself. It requires a new approach to health.

It does not denigrate those who give care. It doesn't place unsavory labels on persons who devote themselves to the care of others. It doesn't call them "facilitators" or "co-dependents," for example. Caregivers have, of late, become suspect. Patients do not trust them to care about them. And some doctors are wary of patients who ask questions because they fear malpractice suits.

The New Caregiver is a person who does not fear patients. That person gives the impression that he or she and the patient are a team composed to discover how the patient's health can be kept at an optimum. It is as important to the practitioner to help patients be healthy as it is to help them overcome an acute medical emergency.

DECISION CONTEXT

It is hard to refuse experimental tests, medication, or surgery when surrounded by a medical milieu. Be sure to take a friend or relative along with you when you suspect an important decision will need to be made.

The American Cancer Society ran an advertisement that read "Cancer is a word, not a sentence." However, when you hear "terminal," "tumor," or "inoperable," you fail to hear further comments. Having a second pair of ears that are less emotionally involved than yours is useful.

When a former client of mine developed cancer, her daughter accompanied her to all her medical treatments. After one particularly painful and confusing treatment at a big hospital where the daughter had to intercede for her weakened mother, the daughter said, "Everyone in the hospital should have a family member in attendance."

In many cultures, that is commonplace. The entire family camps out in the hospital until the sick member is well. In China, for example, medical treatment is divided into categories of urgency. Minor treatments are given at a local clinic in which an air of casualness prevails. I saw male patients playing cards with their cronies while receiving acupuncture treatment for lower back pain. More serious treatments are carried out at the city hospital. Family members are utilized there to perform routine tasks, such as bringing in meals and feeding their sick relatives. Very serious treatment is available at the regional or university hospital. At each of these facilities, the family is welcomed as an adjunct to the healing of the patient.

Despite what our high-tech society can do in medicine, *The New York Times* (April 14, 1991, p. 24) reported that the chances of surviving the first year of life are greater in Shanghai than in New York City.

In the U. S., even when the patient is dying, it is common practice to limit the hours of visitation. The point of whom the facilities are designed to comfort is lost under such restrictions.

I accompanied a friend to a hospital that is known worldwide for its eye specialization. The head doctor there wanted to put my friend on a new medicine. She asked what the side effects were. He told her the medicine occasionally caused psychotic-like episodes and sometimes paralysis.

She drew herself up with dignity and told him that when the medicine was less experimental and the side effects less dangerous, she would consider taking the medicine.

In another case, a client told me of receiving an MRI at the urging of her neurologist and then being told she had multiple sclerosis (MS). Rather than informing her of the research that suggests exercise is helpful in the treatment of MS, the doctor told her there is no cure and she could eventually become a blind invalid.

When the neurologist told my client she had MS, he was in the presence of six doctors in training. Belief in her own sense of self was hard to sustain in such a setting. Particularly when she was alone.

Fighters often tell the doctor they will consider his or her advice and "get back to you." That is the best course of action because it allows the Fighter to make important decisions in surroundings familiar to him or her.

Deciding to have angioplasty while walking in your own garden rather than in a room set up for health emergencies allows you to think about your daily life after the procedure. You may ask yourself, "Will I be able to sit in the sun?" "Will kneeling down to garden be possible?" "Can I carry bushes to transplant them?" "What about digging?"

It is less likely that those questions will occur to you in an unfamiliar milieu. And they are the questions you need to ask your health-care practitioner.

If it is truly impossible to be at home, use your support system to gather items that are familiar to you. They may collect your fuzzy yellow duck, your yoga blanket, your rocks from favorite beaches and bring them to you at the hospital.

Ask some people in your support system to write down questions they would ask in your situation. Your family and friends continue to be in familiar settings where their minds are not influenced by the strange setting. And they know your lifestyle and what is important to you. They know what things you will want to do once you are out of the hospital.

You may want to make out a living will before you are ever sick. In it, you, yourself, will determine what should be done in the event you ever are unable to make decisions. You can decide what extraordinary measures should or should not be used to keep you alive. Some states are required to use those measures if there are no specific signed statements from the sick person.

PATIENTS AS TEACHERS

Patients can train their physicians to trust their instincts as much as their scientific tests. They can do that by modelling their trust of themselves and their own instincts. I always ask my doctor to share his or her hunches with me, just as I have done with them. If they are uncomfortable with my use of the word "hunch," I need to analyze if I feel well served by that practitioner. If the doctor is at ease with the uncertainty of his or her profession, then he or she is at ease with my curiosity about my own body.

There are physicians who do not want to answer questions their patients may ask. That time cannot be billed so unless the physician values the humanity of him or herself as well as the patient, there is no motivation to provide that extra time.

While the team in the hospital is expected to know about whatever issue the patient is dealing with, the patient is frequently expected to know nothing and to ask nothing. However, ignorant patients are becoming scarcer and scarcer. Because of education and television exposés of certain common medical practices, many patients are better informed than they used to be.

In fact, patients may question the doctors they consult as to what medication they are prescribing, why that one, and what side effects are possible. They are more time-demanding than formerly. And they may decide not to follow the advice of the doctor they consult.

Gilda Radner, the comedienne from "Saturday Night Live" who died of cancer, wrote the following poem, published in the New England Journal of Medicine, November 17, 1988:

Gilda Radner on Doctors*

Doctors are whippersnappers
in ironed white coats

Who spy up your rectums and look
down your throats

And press you and poke you with sterilized tools
And stab at solutions that pacify fools.

I used to revere them and do what they said

Till I learned what they learned on was
already dead.

—Gilda Radner

TREATMENT PLANS

Why is it that some doctors' treatment plans are followed slavishly while others are ignored? Not all prescriptions are actu-

---

*Reprinted with permission from the *New England Journal of Medicine*, November 17, 1988.

ally filled, for example. Despite this fact, most people recover from their ailments.

After all, not everyone who was treated with bloodsucking leeches died from the treatment. Doctors often are frustrated by patients' noncompliance with their advice. Much research is devoted to discovering why patients do not comply with treatment advice. It may be for some of the same reasons that make one person a Fatalist and another a Fighter. Does a Fatalist take his medicine and figure it won't do any good anyhow? Or does he or she fail to have prescriptions filled for the same reason—belief that such medication will prove useless?

Fighters do not believe that the only reason they got better was because they took an antibiotic. They do believe that *along with other things* the antibiotic aided in their recovery. The other things may have been humor, Vitamin C, spending time with a friend, talking with relatives.

Often a sense of urgency surrounds making medical decisions. Fatalists tend to forget that they may have been living with the condition for a month or more. Making a decision because "every minute counts" usually means the health practitioner's assessment has more influence than the patient's own. Fighters review the health goals they wrote out before arriving at the medical setting.

"I will not have surgery until all my questions are answered. Those questions need to include the aftermath of surgery. Will I be able to return to work immediately? When? Will I need rehabilitation? How often?"

Will you have your prescriptions filled, for example?

One of the big pharmaceutical companies is conducting research on whether a physician touching a patient has any correlation with the patient's having a prescription filled. They wonder if they can increase their sales by encouraging doctors' caregiving practices. Is a patient's feeling of being cared for, regardless of the medicine used, the main factor in healing?

TOUCH

The touch of the caregiver probably has an impact. A client of mine with a broken foot from a ski accident told me how the doctor had looked with great interest at the X-Rays of her foot but never touched her.

Being physically touched may mean to you that you are touchable. Not being touched may make you feel isolated from other humans.

Does your doctor know what color your eyes are? Are you simply the diabetic, the heart patient, or the cancer victim?

In order for you to feel good with your health-care team, they have to feel good with you. Do you only want them to make you feel better while you give no attention to how they are feeling? Are you annoyed when they don't call you back within a few minutes of your telephoning them on a Saturday night? Do you expect that they will remember what they prescribed for you two months ago without looking at your chart?

Can you answer the following questions? What color are your doctor's eyes? What fabric was the dress she was wearing? What was the pattern of his tie? After all, while you don't want to be identified by your maladies, your doctor doesn't want to be invisible either.

You can touch your doctor in appropriate ways, too. Reaching out to take your doctor's hand when he or she reassures you or tapping him or her on the arm when they say something that amuses you makes the practitioner also feel like a human being.

DESIGNER HEALTH-CARE PRACTITIONERS

Finding a satisfactory physician for you is possible. What is not possible is that your physician can be a miracle worker. He or she is only a consultant *to your own efforts* to live a healthy life.

If you have not received a legacy of a healthy lifestyle, there are ways you can begin to empower yourself for health now. One way is to complete the Health Assessment in Chapter 6. It will enable you to discover in how many ways you allow yourself to be responsible for your own good health. A smoothly running body needs more than cleanliness and food. It needs healthy maintenance.

In response to her question about moving her family from an area where a high tension electric tower crossed her property, a physician colleague asked a patient if she had fastened her seatbelt on her way to his office. You need to ask if you do all you can for yourself instead of waiting for outside forces to tend to you, acting like a newborn who knows his or her parents will feed him or her.

Once you have determined to change some specific health habits, you must be optimistic about your efforts. Unlike Beth James whom you met in Chapter 4, you have to believe that your new habits will be effective. An "It won't make any difference" attitude will hardly spur you on to overcome inertia and the natural reluctance to perform difficult and consistent, sometimes boring, new health habits. You must judge your health from your own former health, not from what a "typical" 35-year-old should be, for instance.

If you have never experienced a sty in your eye, having one is unusual for you. True, it is probably not life-threatening, but it is an indicator that your immune system is not working optimally.

If you wish to strengthen that system, you must make it clear that you are judging yourself by your former health, not by a sort of "generic" patient who shares your age, gender, race, ethnic background, socioeconomic standards, education, and occupation. You want your physician to judge you that way also.

It takes a certain amount of courage to refuse the family legacy of poor health. There may be a tradition in a family that everyone will develop the same malady.

Instead, the similarity can be in making beautiful pie crusts or in being a math whiz. It does not have to be in having poor health.

BONDING

Ultimately, the feelings you have about the person who you have entrusted with the job of working with you to keep you healthy is what keeps you calm when your body is not working up to par.

Reruns of M. A. S. H. show doctors sitting down on the edge of a patient's bed and talking to the patient like a human being. That is the feeling you want to have with your health-care practitioner. You can make that happen with some planning.

Just as a baby and his or her parents take time to bond with each other, it takes time to bond with your health-care team. It also takes unconditional love on the side of each. Without that love flowing in both directions, it is not possible for the trust to develop that is necessary for both parties to want to help each other.

Dr. David Smoot wrote in *Reader's Digest* (Canadian edition, August 1988, p. 55) of his experience in a hospital where he received the best of medical care. No one treated him as a human being who was scared. Finally, at the end of a frightening day, a nurse came into his room to tend to all the issues on her checklist. After straightening the blinds, taking his temperature, giving him his medication, changing the sheets on his bed, she was ready to walk out of the room. Instead she walked over to the sink, dampened a washcloth and sponged his face with it. "This must be very hard for you," she said, before leaving.

ACTIVITIES

1. Write a health chronology of the last six months. Include any changes in your health habits during that time.
2. Ask a friend to roleplay with you your next doctor visit.
3. Write out your health goals.

8

BEATING THE ODDS

You are sitting in your favorite chair in your "rec" room. Dressed in old jogging pants and a T-shirt, you hold a beer in one hand and a bowl of homemade popcorn in your lap. Your other hand absentmindedly strokes your cat's ears. The sound of the clock in the kitchen is heard ticking above the noise of the refrigerator.

On the TV set in front of you, there are people swimming in the ocean. All seems peaceful. Yet the palms of your hands are soaking wet, your heart is beating wildly, and your breathing is shallow.

No matter that you are safely at home, *Jaws* is playing on your TV set and your body believes you are in danger of being attacked by a shark. As a healthy body should, it is preparing to protect you. So, while your mind knows the film is fantasy, your body does not. It believes what it perceives.

From a very early age, bodies respond as they were taught. Children know how their bodies feel. Adults often act as if their bodies are merely envelopes that carry their organs around. Your grown body becomes invisible to you. Speaking of it is not acceptable, in most cultures.

SECONDARY GAINS

However, when you are ill, you are allowed to discuss your
body. No one cuts you off when you discuss how much pain you
feel or how you can't eat. Not since childhood when you said
"poo-poo," "wee-wee," and "snot," have you been allowed to
express bodily functions.

For some people, being free to discuss primitive feelings is a
long-lost delight. They receive the full attention of any group
they are a part of. (They may not be invited again, however.) No
one says, "You're really boring," or "Ugh." Instead, they listen,
respectfully, about each blood test, visit to another specialist,
diet change.

When nothing of interest is happening in someone's life, illness may be the issue he or she can focus on.

In order to refuse the legacy of family illness, you need to
make your body visible to yourself. Rather than ignore the signs
of *dis-ease*, you must return to the feelings of childhood and be
curious and interested in your bodily functions. Not as a topic
for social discussion, but as personal awareness.

Your body may signal you that something is amiss by failing
to sleep well four nights out of seven. Or by having frequent
heartburn.

Just as society has rules about the appropriateness of various
behaviors, the family, which is the foundation of society, has
rules as to what is appropriate, as well.

Studies have shown that different ethnic groups express pain
in ways common to them (Zborowski, 1969). The expression of
pain, therefore, is not a reliable barometer for every patient's
medical status. One patient recovering from gallbladder surgery
may say he is in excruciating pain. Another patient in the same
situation may express little discomfort.

Each family member notes which behaviors receive attention
and which do not. If you descend from a family that gives attention to those who are sick, it is likely that you have learned to
expect attention when you are not in good health. The genogram
you completed (Chapter 2) about caregivers and caretakers will

help you assess the behaviors that received attention in your family.

In order to reject a legacy of inheriting "the family illness," you must follow a strategy designed to help you beat the odds. The following steps can help:

1. Research the family tree as much as possible. Find out the characteristics of both sides of your family. Do relatives live a healthy lifestyle into old age? Are they Fatalists about their health and use that attitude as an excuse to live unhealthy lifestyles?

   Are there many early deaths in the family? Do many people have illness in one area of the body, but not the same illness? Maybe the kidneys are the susceptible organs so there are relatives who have had nephritis, kidney infections, and Wilm's tumor. Knowing such family information is very important.

2. Research the family illness. Some maladies that were impossible to treat just a few years ago have new and more effective treatment plans. Be sure to research alternative methods of healing the malady, not only traditional means. Knowledge of current advances is important and reliance on receiving all new information from one's physician is unrealistic. To learn that no one now dies of breast cancer but rather from its complications is important. So is knowing that having "lumpy breasts" (fibrocystitis) is as natural in the aging process as having wrinkled skin.

3. Assess your own lifestyle. How do you assure your own good health? Now would be a good time to review your Health Assessment from Chapter 6. It is a good guide to what your lifestyle is.

   Why do you deserve to suffer and die young? Do you believe you deserve punishment? Whom will your punishment help?

4. When you listen to your inner self about illness, what do you hear?

   Write your answers down. Answers will be seen by you

alone, so don't hesitate to admit ideas about illness you may know, logically, are incorrect.

Do you think you're destined to be ill and die young (before 55)? Are you deserving to be sick? Why do you deserve such a fate?

Dr. Joan Borysenko (1990) says that most people say "yes" to "Are you being punished for your sins?" They feel, "God is going to get me."

5. Are you unduly impressed by medical advances? Do you obsessively follow every heart transplant and new medication touted on TV or in the newspaper?

Remarkable treatment for rare diseases is facinating, but the maladies suffered by most people—like the common cold—are not always reported on so dramatically. When new advances in medicine are touted, do you feel safer? Does medicine need to develop more and more miracles to overcome your own lack of taking responsibility?

What you decide to do about the five questions above is significant. To beat the odds, you have to play the health game with a full deck.

Does your family have a habit of responding to trouble with vast generalities? "What can you expect of lawyers?" "You never can trust a Hungarian" (or whatever group they are prejudiced against).

What is the long-term effect on the family of the publicity about heart transplants? What happens when bypass surgery patients go home? It is known that as many as half of male bypass recipients never return to work and only 14% of females do (Hall et al., 1983). That unglamorous fact is not publicized.

After considering your answers to these questions, are there any changes you promise yourself to make? Have you reassessed the Health Assessment or are you putting it off until you finish reading or "When I have more time?"

RISK

In families at risk, not *every* member expects to develop the family illness. Some refuse to accept the expectation legacy and live a lifestyle that takes responsibility for good health.

Anne Duffy, 54 (whom you met in Chapter 7), comes from a family in which most female members around the age of 45 have a hysterectomy. Anne was startled and angry when, at her annual checkup, the family gynecologist told her that she would soon be ready to have a hysterectomy. She realized that her physician had inherited the family legacy. He expected Anne to be powerless in the face of the family illness. After all, he had performed hysterectomies on her first cousins, her aunt, and her mother. Despite the fact that Anne's uterus was healthy, he was prepared to think of her as in eventual need of a hysterectomy.

Anne changed her physician and intensified her healthy lifestyle.

She began to walk the eight blocks from the train station to her office. She bought fresh vegetables and learned to cook vegetarian meals and to keep her diet as nutritious as possible. Anne practiced Tai Chi, a Chinese martial art designed to increase energy.

After her three children left home for college and separate lives, Anne realized her lifelong wish of owning a farm. She furnished the barn with two horses and the chicken coop with 12 hens.

Riding horseback and tending to the horses and chickens provided both exercise and a sense of calm. Broadening her social world to include those people with horses and those with chickens provided more fun.

At 54, Anne maintains a healthy uterus and the full intention of keeping herself healthy and intact.

Anne was unwilling to inherit the expectation that she would follow in the footsteps of most of her female relatives. In order to avoid their path, she vigorously follows a lifestyle of good health.

MACHO

Charles McArthur, a factory worker in his 40s, is surrounded by smokers. Charles comes from a family where men smoked heavily, drank lots of coffee and hard liquor, and worked long hours in a factory. They also bit their fingernails. All died by age 50.

Charles's wife urged him to live a different lifestyle as she did not look forward to a life without him.

For Charles to change a learned lifestyle was very difficult. Yet, with the caring of his wife, he began to change. First he gave up smoking, a habit that he had been addicted to since teenage. Charles achieved total cessation of his smoking habit by joining a group program sponsored by his local hospital.

From that accomplishment, he next gave up drinking hard liquor. The men he associated with were heavy drinkers. It took determination not to join them in "a shot and a beer." However, he now can spend an entire evening with them and simply drink two beers.

As he accomplished each of the steps to good health, Charles was reenforced by new dreams of the future. (Men in his family had not dreamt of the future because they were accustomed to believing they had none.) He dreamt of building a cabin in the woods, driving a recreation vehicle across country, and whittling small animals from pieces of wood.

He found that after he had accomplished all of the steps, he stopped chewing his fingernails. He did not wait until retirement to learn to whittle. He began the craft right away. He and his wife started looking for a piece of land on which to build a cabin.

As each goal was met, part of a future dream also became reality. Charles's life became more self-manageable. He gives a lot of credit for his success to his wife's encouragement.

NO HELPER

What can you do if you don't have a caring spouse to encourage your efforts to change a learned lifestyle? It is then even more important to set up specific goals for your future.

When you ask yourself what you are living for, write down the answers that surface. You may write after Goals:

My son's graduation
Seeing my first grandchild
Finishing my master's degree
Building a family cabin in the woods
Taking care of my aging parents
Learning Spanish
Travelling to the country of my grandparents
Tap dancing
Cleaning out the basement
Drawing a family tree for my children

You may add deeper issues:

Becoming more spiritual
Reading about serious subjects
Investigating family stories of "weird" events

Whatever your goals, they are your motivation to live. Without motivation, each day will feel like any other. You will not have the commitment to be well if you have no future goals.

If you continue to feel you need outside help to develop your goals, you may want to join a support group or begin therapy.

In Appendix B on Family Illnesses, there is a listing of genetic counselors and genetic support groups. A note or call to them will provide information on support groups.

Your local hospital or Mental Health Society will also give you information on how to be in touch with others who are facing similar problems.

Attendance once or twice will allow you to discover if this group is one you want to join.

The same is true of therapy. A few sessions will tell you if you and the therapist work well in developing future goals for you.

GUILT

It may be hard to develop future goals when you are feeling guilty about the present. As noted in Chapter 5, under Blame, there are those who are not compassionate towards a sick person because they blame him or her for the condition. That may even be the attitude of the sick person—"I brought this on myself."

There are those who believe that the flip side of being responsible for staying healthy or recovering from an illness is being guilty of developing the illness in the first place. They ask themselves and their friends who are sick what they are getting out of the illness. They do not believe in environmental causes of illness. Nor do they believe in accidents. Everything is chosen— parents, schooling, economic stratum.

The significant word is *responsible*, not *guilty.* You are responsible for maintaining good health and for using your personal powers to recover from illness. You are not guilty of developing an illness, since you usually do not consciously decide in advance to be ill. However, you may have been unfortunate enough to live in a family that fatalistically believed nothing could be done to alter the future.

If you fatalistically await to "see what happens," you often do not take responsibility for adopting any personal steps to aid your recovery. Those people who have such attitudes often were programmed as children to expect that their fate was sealed.

Guilt is a heavy and needless burden to carry. It is very difficult to assume personal responsibility for a foolish action you have committed. To assume personal responsibility not only for one's own poor health but for the poor health of one's children and grandchildren is extremely weighty and unnecessary.

That was the case with Dave Black's mother, Edith. She had

debilitating arthritis and when her son showed signs of the illness, Edith lamented that she had given her heirs a legacy of arthritis. In the time she spent lamenting, Edith could have researched what new treatments are available for the illness. Instead she felt guilty.

Because of sayings you heard as a child, you believe yourself to be powerless to avoid developing illness. You must believe you can develop wellness by using that same power source.

MENTAL AWARENESS

Awareness, rather than guilt, is the first step toward illness prevention. The more you know about your family health history, the better equipped you will be to avoid pitfalls that may have affected other family members.

One way to observe the complete picture of your family health history is through use of a genogram which you have already drawn in Chapter 2.

In charting your family tree, you might note that a particular condition such as hypertension, for example, shows up with some frequency. Armed with this knowledge, you can take steps to avoid developing the problem yourself.

First, however, you need to make a positive commitment to refuse your family illness legacy and establish a firm belief in your ability to do so. Without faith and determination, your good intentions to alter your lifestyle are likely to evaporate.

"If people make behavioral changes without changing their internal values, beliefs, and attitudes, the new behaviors are less likely to stick when the external supports disappear," says Dr. Lawrence W. Green (1988), a leading specialist in health promotion and former director of the Center for Health Promotion Research and Development at the University of Texas.

Dr. Green cites "internal conversion" as a factor essential to bring about lasting change. In other words, before you are likely to maintain successful lifestyle changes, you must make mind changes. He believes that desirable alteration in health-damaging behavior often results from a combination of beliefs in susceptibility, severity of consequences, and benefits that outweigh costs, but even more important is the squaring of the behavior with more deep-seated values.

Fatalists expect that hypertension, heart disease, cancer, diabetes, or some other illness will "happen" to them because it runs in the family.

Change begins with the conscious affirmation that you are in control of your own health. What you do or don't do—smoke, drink, rest, play, exercise, overwork, overeat, skip meals, pop pills, take drugs—is your decision and affects your physical condition. You decide yourself. Nothing and no one forces you. You are in control.

You must believe that by relinquishing unhealthy habits, substituting healthy ones, and adopting health-preserving behavior you can protect and improve your physical condition. In effect, you can refuse the family illness and beat the odds of developing and dying from it.

BODILY AWARENESS

In order to accomplish these changes, you must be in touch with how your body feels. You must add to awareness of your family history the awareness of sensory responses.

Boys are taught to "Grin and bear it" and that "Big boys don't cry." They are not encouraged to listen to the language of their bodies. Instead, their bodies notify them dramatically of health problems. As adults, these same boys tend to minimize chest pain by calling it indigestion. It is not until the chest pain becomes a full-blown heart attack that it is acknowledged.

Men can overcome this weakness by accepting a version of themselves that includes feelings as being manly.

Men, as evidenced by crying soldiers who had just seen a comrade die in Desert Storm, do have feelings. Those feelings can influence fatalism or powerfulness. It makes sense to feel grief for dead comrades, even though grief was not openly expressed in one's family.

Some men and women who descend from families having frequent early deaths cannot imagine any way to beat the odds of such a legacy. They may await the first symptoms of illness as others await the first signs of Spring. They are not surprised when they appear.

They ask themselves, "Why go to the effort to refuse the family legacy of early death and illness when there is no assurance the effort will succeed?"

The question is best answered by those who have made the effort despite a family history that boded poorly for good health. One such person is Mickey Mantle, the former Yankee outfielder who is now in the Baseball Hall of Fame.

For three generations, the men in Mantle's family died before the age of 40. All of them suffered from Hodgkins Disease, an illness that affects the lungs.

Unlike the males in the generations before him, Mickey Mantle worked outdoors. He didn't smoke. They did. Mickey Mantle also scheduled time to play. His male relatives did not.

Have Mantle's efforts succeeded? Today, approaching 60, he shows no signs of Hodgkins Disease.

Yet he says in his autobiography, *The Mick* (1985), "I often wondered why the disease had skipped me after it had felled so many in my family."

Famous people may seem unique. You give yourself excuses about not having much money. "I'd do that too if I had all the money he has." "After all, he has the best medical advice in the world."

Consider Liz Carmichael, 52, a former client whose husband left her after 28 years of marriage. Liz's family has a history of diabetes. Because that history casts a shadow over her life, Liz made certain to follow a healthy diet, to keep her weight within normal limits, to exercise regularly. For six months following her husband's leaving, however, Liz allowed her depression to override her good habits. She ate much ice cream, stopped walking, and gained weight.

One of Liz's grandchildren, a four-year-old, told her one day that she was getting as fat as Santa Claus. That comment stopped Liz's self destructive mode. She returned to her health regimen the same day.

After attending a workshop on family illness, Althea Miller decided to reclaim her power to be free of high blood pressure.

Althea is a 26-year-old black woman who descends from a family of hypertensives. Althea knows that high blood pressure is a common health hazard for blacks. Her sister weighs over 200 pounds and so does her mother.

Following a path no one in her family pursued, Althea began to meditate regularly. In meditation, she visualized herself as a slim, sexy woman playing tennis in a short, white tennis skirt that showed off her slender but athletic legs.

Then Althea joined a gym. Each night after work she exercised in the company of other people.

Because she lives at home, Althea found it difficult to change her diet from her family's accustomed fare. The hardest part of her regimen was to persuade her sister and mother to help her maintain a low weight. But Althea did so. They helped her plan a menu each week that was low in fats and salt. Not only has Althea maintained her weight, but her sister and mother have lost weight as well. Althea now laughingly refers to herself as "The Great Black Hope."

HUMOR

The power of humor to unseat disease is great. In his book *Anatomy of an Illness* (1979), Norman Cousins recounted how laughter helped him regain his health when nothing else was effective. I have added to sources of laughter taken from Duke University's Comprehensive Cancer Center which Norman Cousins provided in his book, *Head First* (1989):

Books

Author	*Title*
Allen, Woody	Without Feathers
Angelou, Maya	I Know Why the Caged Bird Sings
Baker, Russell	The Rescue of Miss Yaskell and Other Pipe Dreams

Bloch, Arthur	Murphy's Law
Bloch, Arthur	Murphy's Law Book Two
Blount, Roy, Jr.	Crackers
Bombeck, Erma	The Grass Is Always Greener over the Septic Tank
Boynton, Sandra	Chocolate: The Consuming Passion
Breathed, Berke	Penquin Dreams: And Stranger Things
Breathed, Berke	Bloom County
Buchwald, Art	You Can Fool All of the People All of the Time
Buchwald, Art	The Bollo Caper
Burns, George	Dr. Burns' Prescription for Happiness
Burns, George	Dear George
Camp, Joe	Oh Heavenly Dog!
Combs, Ann	Helter Shelter
Cuppy, Will	Decline and Fall of Practically Everybody
Davis, Jim	The Fourth Garfield Treasury
Diller, Phyllis	The Complete Mother
Dwyer, Bill	Dictionary for Yankees
Ephron, Delia	How to Eat Like a Child: And Other Lessons in Not Being a Grown-up
Evans, Greg	Is it Friday Yet, Luann?
Fields, W. C.	I Never Met a Kid I Liked
Gately, George	Heathcliff Smooth Sailing
Greenburg, Dan	How to Make Yourself Miserable
Grizzard, Lewis	Don't Sit Under the Grits Tree with Anyone Else but Me
Hewlett, John	The Blarney Stone
Horn, Maurice	Comics of the American West
Keillor, Garrison	Happy to Be Here
Kerr, Jean	Please Don't Eat the Daisies
Larson, Gary	The Far Side Gallery Two
MacNelly, Jeff	The Greatest Shoe on Earth
Millar, Jeff, and Hinds, Bill	Tank McNamara
Ohman, Jack	Drawing Conclusions: A Collection of Political Cartoons
Pizzuto, John	The Great Wall Street Joke Book
Peter, Laurence J.	The Laughter Prescription
Powell, Dwane	The Reagan Chronicles
Schulman, Max	Rally Round the Flag, Boys!

Smith, Wes   Welcome to the Real World
Viorst, Judith   It's Hard to Be Hip Over Thirty and Other
                          Tragedies of Married Life
Wilde, Larry   The Official Executive's Joke Book
Wilder, Roy, Jr.   You All Spoken Here
Winters, Jonathan   Mouse Breath Conformity and Other Social
                          Ills

AUDIOCASSETTES

Performer   *Title*

Anonymous   Bloopers
Clower, Jerry   The Ambassador of Goodwill
Clower, Jerry   Live from the Stage of the Grand Ole Opry
Clower, Jerry   Top Gum
Clower, Jerry   The One and Only
Clower, Jerry   Runaway Truck
Clower, Jerry   Live in Picayune
Cosby, Bill   The Best of Bill Cosby
Cosby, Bill   Is a Very Funny Fellow, Right!
Cosby, Bill   Wonderfulness
Cosby, Bill   Inside the Mind Of
Cosby, Bill   200 M. P. H.
Dangerfield, Rodney   I Don't Get No Respect
Fields, W. C.   The Best of W. C. Fields
Gardner, Gerald   All the President's Wits
Marx, Groucho   The Works
Keillor, Garrison   News from Lake Wobegon-Fall
Keillor, Garrison   News from Lake Wobegon-Spring
Keillor, Garrison   News from Lake Wobegon-Summer
Keillor, Garrison   News from Lake Wobegon-Winter
Nash, Ogden   Ogden Nash Reads
Rivers, Joan   What Becomes a Semi-Legend Most?
Stevens, Ray   Crackin' Up
Stevens, Ray   Greatest Hits
Stevens, Ray   Surely You Joust
Stevens, Ray   He Thinks He's Ray Stevens

VIDEOCASSETTES
Adventure

Cool Hand Luke   Jeremiah Johnson

"Crocodile" Dundee   Jewel of the Nile
High Road to China   Patton
Jake Speed   Raiders of the Lost Ark
Raise the Titanic!   Silverado
Rocky III   Superman
Romancing the Stone   Top Gun

Classics

The Bridge on the   On Golden Pond
    River Kwai   To Kill a Mockingbird
Casablanca
From Here to
    Eternity

Humor/Comedy

Airplane!   Privates on Parade
All of Me   The Return of the Pink Panther
Back to the Future   Silverado
Blazing Saddles   Some Like It Hot
The Films of Laurel   Volunteers
and Hardy   What About Bob?
Making Mr. Right   When Harry Met Sally
The Making of the   48 Hours
Stooges   Fried Green Tomatoes
Driving Miss Daisy
City Slickers
The Money Pit

Musicals

The Jolson Story   42nd Street
Jolson Sings Again   White Nights
The Sound of Music   Rick Springfield

Science Fiction

Star Wars
Star Trek IV: The
    Voyage Home

Westerns

The Alamo   True Grit
Shane   Hang 'em High

Documentaries
 National
   Geographic-Iceland

Being able to laugh at your illness and the other stresses of your life allows you to keep the difficulties in perspective. Part of your family legacy may be to view illness, especially the family illness, with great seriousness. It may be necessary for you to disclaim that legacy.

CHANGING HABITS

As Althea Miller and others who have inherited unhealthy habits know, change can be difficult. Old habits are hard to break, and efforts at habit alteration require a plan. The successful implementation of a plan depends on five things that I call the Acorn Effect: Assessment, Choice, Optimism, Resolve, and New goals.

1. *You must assess your current habits. Decide which ones adversely affect your health.*

   Assessing your health habits can be done by reviewing your Health Assessment (Chapter 6). What three items that you marked "never" are you determined to change? Choose a date by which you will accomplish the change. Remind yourself of your commitment by a series of colored circles in places that will help. For example, place a blue circle on your car's control panel to remind you to fasten your seatbelt, a yellow circle on the refrigerator to remind you of your commitment to diet, and a green circle on your watch to remind you to laugh at least once an hour.

2. *You must choose to change. The choice must be your own and not dependent on what someone else wants for you.* Choosing to change is not easy to do. Use all the aids you can to assist you.

   Encourage a support system in or outside your family to

buoy up your determination. Make a date with a friend to walk several times a week. Or share low-calorie recipes with another friend.

3. *You must be optimistic about your efforts. They will result in a longer and healthier life.*

    Congratulate yourself on your accomplishments towards good health. Put pictures of yourself at your best on your desk or in another prominent place. Get photos of your oldest relative to place alongside the favorite ones of you. Celebrate your successes. Go to your favorite restaurant to mark your one-month anniversary of ending smoking.

4. *You must resolve to develop health-producing habits. Commitment to maintain your efforts is necessary.* Much has been written on what habits cause good health. Read some of them. A listing of a few is given in this book's Bibliography.

    Once you have an overview of what habits actually produce good health, decide which ones you will follow. Ask yourself if a habit is intrinsically health-producing.

    You can give yourself mini-rewards. For every 100 miles you walk, you can make one long distance phone call to a friend who has moved across the country, for example.

5. *You must establish new health goals and be determined to achieve them.* Do not sabotage your efforts with vague dreams of your future. Instead make strong and specific goals. Enunciate strong comments to yourself frequently throughout the day, i.e., "Strut your stuff."

    A person who inherits a particular genetic health condition or is susceptible or predisposed to certain illnesses can withstand any illness better if he or she possesses an attitude of hope. You can make a difference in your physical health. It is worth the effort.

The most significant change in U.S. health care over the last decade has been that heart disease has decreased (Killip, 1985). At the same time, the national average expenditure for running shoes has increased. More people exercise, have eliminated fats, sugar, and salt from their diets, stopped smoking, practice stress management.

Jack Latham, a former client, descends from a family in which his mother died at 39 of heart disease. His father, now 63, has a history of angina pectoris. Several of Jack's uncles died in their 40s of heart disease.

Jack gave up smoking when he turned 30. Changing the rest of his lifestyle was harder. A plumber, Jack was given to taking quick food breaks at fast-food spots between jobs. Not only was his diet made up of foods loaded with fat, salt, and sugar, but the food was also packed with empty calories. Jack had gained many pounds from his diet.

To change bad eating habits was not easy. Jack began to place a bag of snacks—carrots, celery, unsalted peanuts—on the front seat of his truck. On his visits to fast-food stops, he ordered black decaffinated coffee. In that way, he continued the social life to which he was accustomed at the places he was used to.

Jack's work as a plumber required much hard work and his muscle tone was in good shape. Now that he was also slimmer, his chances of having an early heart attack were greatly lessened.

CONTEXT AFFECTIVE HABITS

In my practice, I find that some heavy smokers are totally unwilling to give up the habit. They say they must smoke. Yet, research shows that smokers have no difficulty refraining from the habit while in theaters, churches, or workplaces that prohibit smoking. They do not experience the urge to smoke when the context does not allow it. However, when the same people moved to a context that did allow smoking, they felt the urge to light up.

Placing limits on where you can smoke helps to decrease and finally eliminate smoking. For example, one woman told me she allowed herself to smoke outdoors only. In midwinter, she had to don a coat and go outdoors to smoke. The limit she placed on herself eventually allowed her to eliminate smoking entirely.

The change in context of where, when, and how you perform unhealthy habits is significant. Recapturing your power to create your lifestyle is very potent.

Ask yourself if the context has become habitual.

A former client, Joyce Simpson, found that whenever she studied for her classes in graduate school she ate toast slathered with butter and jelly. She realized she used to eat this food when she studied in high school. The context of studying was the same and fostered her body's memory of "study food."

She began to study at the desk in her bedroom rather than at the dining room table as she had done in high school. Changing the context also changed the automatic eating she had been doing.

I experience the same result at the start of Lent. Before the Lenten season begins, I rarely think of food. I simply eat when I am hungry or when everyone else around me is eating.

However, during Lent, I promise not to snack between meals. I note when my next meal will be. And when it is time for the meal, I eat more than I am hungry for. I am so concerned that I will be hungry before the next meal that I anticipate hunger before I feel it.

Fear of developing illness is like that. A person can anticipate having a family illness despite the fact that the illness is not hereditary (even if it were, not everyone in the family will get it) and even though they have no symptoms of it.

An attitude of hope is essential to good health. Helplessness in the face of a possiblity of danger uses one's energy in the service of fear.

ENERGY

Energy is replenishable. Often we find ourselves tolerating a situation that drains our energy—like a phone call from someone who is always down-in-the-mouth. Rather than saying, "I can't talk right now," we endure the call and then feel sluggish for the next hour.

We sometimes ration those events that make us feel on top of the world. If a call to a certain friend always results in our feeling better, we may put off making such a call by saying, "I don't want to make a pest of myself."

Yet, we provide endless amounts of time for persons or events who tire us. We often run on empty until our bodies are kind enough to give us an illness as an excuse. Because of the illness, we can make excuses that are acceptable to others. With a winter flu, we can say, "My ears are all clogged up. I can't hear you. Let me call you when I feel better." The draining person will soon find someone else to listen to his or her complaints.

During the gasoline crisis some years ago, my usual filling station was sometimes out of gasoline. Without a moment's hesitation, I drove across the street and bought gas there.

As a family therapist, I've discovered the same thing. Sometimes, a would-be client leaves a message for me to call immediately. I call as soon as I receive the message, but the line may be busy whenever I attempt to reach him or her. The person finds other options besides me when in need. That keeps me humble and the client empowered.

Energy has to be kept at a constant level of effectiveness. Without that level, ennui sets in.

At a dinner party I gave, the physicist husband of one of my therapist friends interrupted a lengthy conversation about schizophrenia by saying, "This conversation is very boring. Can we change it?"

The other guests sat stunned for a minute and then began conversations on livelier subjects of more general interest.

My friend had the courage to guard his energy level. He was unwilling to deplete it, but wanted to increase it. His comment allowed growth to occur.

The ultimate solution for beating the odds of early death through illness is to assess your energy level. Since energy is replenishable, we can learn to use it for our health. Without energy, we grow weary of life.

"It is too much of an effort."

With limitless amounts of energy, life is never too much of an effort.

The following chart will allow you to assess what you do with energy. Do you allow it to fade away or do you actively increase it?

I suggest you complete the following short exercise. If you are a dyed-in-the-wool Fatalist about your health, you won't do it. After all, to be a true Fatalist means you don't believe change can occur.

ENERGY CHARTS

Energy Depletion Chart

On a piece of unlined paper draw four columns.

Title the first column, *Family*; the second, *Friends*; the third, *Work*; and the fourth, *Other*. Title the chart *Energy Depletion* (Table 1).

Now ask yourself: After sharing what events with which members of my family do I feel as if I am tired and in need of a rest? For example, if I talk with my mother on the phone, do I feel exhausted? If I discuss clothes with my teenaged daughter, am I tired? After Thanksgiving dinner with my Aunt Mae, am I wiped out for a week?

Table 1.
Energy Depletion

Family	*Friends*	*Work*	*Other*
1. Thanksgiving Dinner	1. Shopping with my best friend	1. At Christmas Party	1. At cocktail party
2. Shopping with my mother-in-law	2. Talking to my friends on the phone	2. New sales manager	2. At art exhibits
3. Talking on the phone with my cousin, Mert	3. Visiting a former close friend	3. My boss—especially when he acts all-knowing	3. At New Year's Eve parties
4. Funerals	4. Listening to the family problems of Janice	4. At budget meetings—especially when I have to justify costs	
5. Visits to sick relatives			

You may find that a family member you enjoy in one setting drains you of energy in another. A cousin you have fun shopping with may also be exhausting when you meet her at family dinners. Be honest with yourself. Write down all the instances that make you tired, physically. List in Column One, *Family*, all the events and people in your family that sap your energy.

Now move to Column Two, *Friends*. Ask yourself: When I'm with which friends, doing what, do I feel energyless? After I am with my best friend shopping, do I feel fatigued? After talking with an old friend, do I feel that I need a rest? When I return from a vacation with a group of buddies, do I feel ready to sleep for a month?

Place all those people and settings under Column Two.

Proceed to Column Three, *Work*. After what work experience or with which colleagues am I in need of a break? What happens after I meet with my board of directors, my division manager, my boss, my secretary? How do I feel after staff meetings, task force meetings, planning sessions, budget meetings? Write all those instances under Column Three.

Column Four, *Other*, may surprise you. You may find you are weary after church socials or parties celebrating political victories—events that you consider fun. Write them all down.

Energy Sources Chart

On another unlined piece of paper draw the same four columns titled *Energy Sources* (Table 2).

On this page you will record what gives you energy instead of what depletes you of it. Maybe you'll find that shopping with your sister, skiing with your cousin, baking cookies with your mother represent events and members of your family that energize you. List them under Column One, *Family*. Under Column Two, *Friends*, consider where and with which friends you feel rejuvenated. Sharing jokes with a former college roommate, playing touch football with a group of neighbors, having a beer with a friend after work, telephoning long distance to a high-school buddy may all provide you with energy. Note all of them under Column Two.

Column Three, *Work*, is where you can list what work events and people involved renew you. Finishing a group project, receiving praise for a completed job, having lunch with the maintenance crew, talking with an old client. List all those happenings under Column Three.

Again, in Column Four, *Other*, you may discover some surprises. Here you might list watching the sun set behind a group of office buildings, hearing the sound of the Angelus bell from the church on the corner, smelling fir trees or freshly baked bread. (One of the things that refreshes me is the smell of shavings in a pencil sharpener.)

Now lay the two sheets of paper next to each other in front of you. Which things do you believe you can't change in the first column of Page One, *Family*? The people or the events that drain you.

Must you talk to your mother when she calls every night at dinnertime?

"Yes. Poor thing. She has nothing interesting in her life. The least I can do is listen to her complaints."

What about constantly demanding that your teenager straighten his room? Will he become a derelict if he grows up with a messy room?

You may reply: "Those things are important. They make young people develop good habits."

Before an impending holiday, you may reminisce: "The last two Thanksgivings have been awful. I don't want to listen again to my mother talk about what dress she wants to be buried in." Are you willing to interrupt conversations about unpleasant, repetitious topics or do you feel helpless to create change?

You can change the family legacy of endurance. You do not have to tolerate anything you experience from a family member.

Consider the next column on Page One, *Friends*.

Can I tell my best friend that we always do my shopping last after we have used up all our enthusiasm with her needs?

Can I say that we have talked enough about problems and I'd like to discuss something that is fun?

Can I beg off some activities on a hectic vacation and just stay in my room and read a book?

All those things require empowering yourself and not being afraid that you will lose your friends if you assert yourself. Maybe you didn't learn how to act with self-esteem in your family. You may have to learn it now.

When you compare how you lose energy with friends with how you gain it, you may notice that you simply wait for good events to happen. You wait for one of your neighbors to suggest a game of touch football. You meet with college roommates when one of them calls and suggests you return to the campus for Alumni Day. Your friend at aerobics class says, "How about meeting after work for a beer?" You can decide to take the initiative in suggesting experiences that energize you.

It's time now to consider how you lose and gain energy from *Work*.

On your job, do you receive praise and/or pay increases for work well done?

If you are a school teacher, does the principal make your efforts public? Is your photo taken and placed in the school newsletter?

If you are a librarian, are your efforts at research into literature on a certain topic cited at the start of the published book?

Do you receive phone calls in your area of expertise? Are you recognized for excellence?

Are you the worker everyone blames for the project being late or who doesn't help the team?

Is it at your desk where there is always someone telling a sad tale of his or her life? Are you the unofficial "company social worker"?

The final category, *Other*, may also reveal much information. You may receive energy from watching waves hit the beach or watching children play. Being listened to as you tell a funny story may uplift you.

Attending required cocktail parties or trudging through an art

Table 2.
Energy Sources

Family	Friends	Work	Other
1. Thanksgiving Dinner	1. Shopping with my best friend	1. Being acknowledged for work well done	1. At a good movie
2. Talking on the phone with my cousin, Mert	2. Going for walk with Andy	2. My secretary	2. At a good play
3. Being funny telling about family events	3. Laughing with childhood friend	3. The "team"	3. Seeing a pretty sunset
4. Getting together with cousin Bridget and her daughter	4. Reminiscing	4. Having my picture taken for publication in the quarterly newsletter	4. Watching kids play
5. Looking at her family photo album with my cousin, Mildred	5. Seeing friends with their grown children and grandchildren		5. Christmas
6. Receiving old photos from my cousin, Tom			

show may drain you of energy. How do you ensure keeping a high level of energy?

When we lay the two sheets beside each other, we can see what is different about those people or things that build our energy. How does each chart differ from the other? What patterns do you see emerging?

Under *FAMILY* and *FRIENDS*, do you find similarities?

Do you passively wait for someone to send you a note or call you? Would you do the same about food and sleep? Do you wait until someone serves you a meal before you eat? Does someone put you in your nightclothes and to bed before you go to sleep?

If you are passive about what happens with Family and Friends, do you find that the events and people who build your energy are initiated from the outside, or do you actively invite them into your daily existence?

Please stop your reading now and consider ways to increase your energy. You need to make a commitment to yourself for doing those things that support you.

One of the things that can support you is to make an audiotape that you can play whenever you need help with your health image. On the tape, you may mention all the comments you didn't hear as a child.

HEALTH TAPE

Before you make the tape, write out all the health comments you can think of. For example, you might want to include:

"You poor baby."
"Take it easy."
"Don't get up too quickly."
"Give yourself a rest."
"Don't be so hard on yourself."
"Enjoy poor health."
"I know you'll be as good as new soon."
"You'll be okay in a few days."

One of my colleagues, who is very tall and handsome, made a tape of 27 minutes of applause. When he needs it, he walks nude throughout his apartment and keeps bowing to the unknown audience. By the end of the tape, he feels much better.

The point is that the tape must be significant to you. In an effort to be well, you must attain body awareness. That awareness develops from a sensitivity to your own body signals.

Some people totally ignore body signals. You may have chest pains, your skin color becomes gray, your sleep is disrupted, you gain weight. But you refuse to respect your body signals.

Even when someone says, "You don't look well. Are you

okay?" you brush them off. You continue to live as you've been living without altering anything in your lifestyle. The care and reverence you need to adopt to be well is missing.

The goals of good health and long life alone are not enough to counter-balance the hard work of being healthy. If you run each day merely to look younger than your peers or stay slim so you can show off your svelte body at your high school class reunion, the efforts will probably be too difficult to sustain.

The goals of good health and long life are only one-third of a person's make-up. Mind, body, and spirit need to be in balance in order to give one the feeling of happiness. A healthy body, a vigorous mind, and a zestful spirit must co-exist.

What would you do with a life free from the fear of illness?

HEALTHY LIVES

If you are truly likely to develop a family illness, how influenced are you by the myth that you are powerless in the face of its threat?

Do you know for sure what your chances are of developing the family illness? Are you basing your fears on what someone told you years ago? Do you have current information on the transmittability and treatment of the illness? Do you know, for example, that 95 percent of those with Hodgkin's Disease now have been symptom-free for at least five years?

Some information stays rooted in time despite new research on it.

People with a family history of illness find it difficult to practice good health habits. After all, they ask, why go to the trouble when my efforts will probably prove useless?

Why, indeed?

The reason for following healthy habits is that there is disagreement about what percentage of illness is hereditary. Even with hereditary illnesses, only some family members develop it. There is no known way to predetermine which members are certain to develop any illness. The belief that you are powerless in the face of the family illness is absurd.

Accepting a family legacy and its accompanying myth of powerlessness when you can voluntarily disinherit yourself takes determination. You can be determined when you surround yourself with a support system that is as determined as you hope to be. That determination will multiply your efforts to live a long and healthy life.

ACTIVITIES

1. Make a commitment to yourself about learning what people or events deplete you of energy. After doing the Energy Charts ask a friend or family member if you can send them three postcards reporting on what events or people drain you of energy. Send the first card three weeks from now, the second at six weeks, and the third at the end of two months.
2. Listen to positive comments given children for the next few weeks and then write up an outline for the contents of your tape. Make a date with yourself for making a health tape.

9

IMPLICATIONS FOR THERAPISTS

The saying, "Step on a crack; break your mother's back" was popular when I was in elementary school. I remember stepping on a sidewalk crack on my way home from school to prove I wasn't superstitious. I then rushed home to be sure my mother's back was okay. Despite the fact that no one truly believed the saying, I can still feel the flood of relief that engulfed my body when I saw my mother was just as I left her.

A child hearing that "All the Harris men die before 40 of heart attacks" or "All the Hyland women die of breast cancer" is seriously influenced by what he or she has heard. Therapists can help clients decrease the power of such sayings.

REASON FOR THERAPY

Those sayings are important in many aspects of adults' lives. They influence physical as well as mental health. What people have heard years earlier still influences them when as parents they seek out a family therapist to help them with a troublesome teenager or an emotionally distant parent. Yet they are often impatient with a therapist who probes into questions that include values taught by repetitive sayings.

One family of five who consulted me, the Spooners, sought

help when one of their teenagers, Arthur, continually ran afoul of the law.

With the entire family at the initial interview, I drew a genogram as we spoke. It was evident that the males in the family died by the age of 50 of sudden heart attacks.

When I saw that the father was 49, I turned to the "acting out" son and thanked him for bringing his family for therapy.

No one was more surprised by my comment than Arthur. He definitely did not want to be thanked for anything. A surly, unkempt 16-year-old boy, Arthur wanted to be known as a problem, not as a saviour.

His family was as reluctant as he was to see him as providing anything good for them.

I explained that my hunch was that everyone in the family was afraid that the father would soon die. Yet, no one knew how to talk about their fears.

Like a burst dam, the father began to spill out the fact that when he was Arthur's age his own father died of a sudden heart attack. His teenage rebelliousness was cited by his mother as the cause of his father's death: "You were the death of him."

We discussed the health habits of Mr. Spooner's father. His father smoked three packs of cigarettes a day, was overweight and sedentary. His job as a trucker was filled with stress.

Mr. Spooner realized his father was responsible for his own health. He no longer held himself responsible for his father's death and vowed to discontinue telling Arthur, "You'll be the death of me."

The burden of responsibility for someone else's health is an enormous one. Without thought, it can be verbally draped over a child's shoulders and never lifted, even into adulthood.

Allowing the Spooner family to recognize that each member was responsible for his or her own actions was the first step to emotional and physical health. They needed to have help in designing a picture of the future as well as in developing encouraging sayings.

One way I helped the Spooners at another session was to guide them in the creation of a new design for their family. I asked each of them to choose six pictures they responded to from a pile of magazines I gave them. (Usually dysfunctional families have had little experience of such a joint activity.)

FAMILY COLLAGE

I put a pile of magazines and a number of scissors on the floor and told the Spooners to each pick six pictures, color or black and white, that they would like to see themselves as or a picture they would like to be in. After telling them they had 10 minutes in which to complete the assignment, I set a clock in a prominent spot.

The assignment forced the verbal dominators to be quieted. I helped the young children rather than have their parents give up their alloted time helping them. (Parents in an enmeshed family frequently ignore their own needs to attend to the needs of their children.)

When the pictures were assembled, I asked each family member to choose one picture from the six he or she had selected for them to make a family collage. I provided a large piece of poster board to mount them on and asked them to design a family picture.

One picture included two adults on a beach—placid water, palm trees, tanned bodies, no other people. Another was of a child eating a chocolate ice cream cone. A third was of a young adult woman dressed in a grey pinstriped suit with a white blouse fastened with a silk bow at the neck. Another was of a football player in full regalia, his face showing sweat beneath the black smudges under his eyes. The fifth picture was of a sneaker. The final picture was a copy of a Norman Rockwell painting depicting a family at Thanksgiving, the grandmother's hair in a bun fastened at the nape of her neck, the children's freckles obvious and the parents smiling broadly.

The resulting collage, after much discussion about its arrangement, provided a future goal for the family.

The questions I asked after the family picture was completed included:

1. Why did you choose this picture? Let's see your other choices.
2. In what ways do you see your picture having a positive effect on the family?
3. How do you see the family having a positive effect on you?
4. How do you see the family having a negative effect on you?
5. How do you see yourself as depicted in that picture having a negative effect on the family?
6. Whose picture pleases you the most?
7. Whose picture disturbs you the most?
8. What do you imagine the other members of the family miss about you if they see you only this way? Which aspects of you will they fail to know?
9. Do you have a second picture you would like to add to the family collage?"

Then I gave each family member the opportunity to add one of his or her five other pictures to the collage.

I again asked the same questions, except for the last one.

Finally, I asked each family member what he or she thought the strengths and weaknesses of such a family would be. This gave each of them an opportunity to stand aside and act as observers of this fictitious family. But the fiction was of their own making.

PERSONAL DESIGNS

I think it is important for therapists to help families recognize that they design their future. They are not at the mercy of outside events, most of the time.

The significance of the family collage technique with families influenced by the expectation of inheriting family illnesses is that it provides them with the experience of seeing themselves as they would like to be rather than as they are portrayed by others.

One of the most difficult tasks for people to face is predicting their future. They may dread the future, but never speak of the events they fear will happen.

Therapists need to ask family members why they will not follow other relatives' journeys into bad health. "I just won't." "I follow healthy habits." "I'm like my mom. It's my dad's family that is unhealthy."

Help your clients be specific. Tell them the answer is too vague for you to understand their precise meaning.

To "I just won't," ask why they won't. What about them is unlike the family of origin?

Keep returning to specifics.

During a two-day seminar I ran for women in a university graduate program, I asked them to tell me at the end of the first day what situation they would find when they arrived home that evening. The graduate students resisted the question.

Ultimately, they followed my request and each wrote down on a card to be seen by her alone what she expected to find when she arrived home.

The following morning each student reread what she had predicted. They were all correct.

One had predicted the baby would have a wet diaper which her husband had not changed. Another predicted there would be no dinner prepared. Another foretold that her husband would have set the dining room table with candles and flowers and have a meal prepared. Two women who lived with their mother predicted she would be ironing their blouses when they arrived home.

Women generally are resourceful in the face of problems. Predicting what those problems will be is not common procedure for them.

The graduate students had never been asked to predict something in their personal lives. Being able to do so effected a significant change in their sense of power.

STORYTELLING

I ask client families to share with each other the stories that they remember. Such stories are future determiners.

"When Grandma came down with the coughing, we all knew her days were numbered." A woman who told her family that remembrance was terrified when her young daughter began to cough from pneumonia.

Before an operation, saying "Only 11 percent of those receiving this operation survive" may have a negative influence on a client. Have clients change that to, "I will recover from this operation."

When clients share the belief that they, too, will get the family illness, the therapist can help them redesign such comments to make them positive. There are many good books on how to do so. *Getting Well Again* by the Simontons is one of the best.

GOAL-SETTING

People in general have never learned to set goals at home. Yet they routinely set goals at school or work. Their experience does not include goal-setting for their personal lives. A therapist can open up new avenues for the future by treating clients as if they are capable not only of setting goals but of reaching them.

Mr. Spooner, whom we met at the beginning of this chapter, responded to my initial comments about health by telling me, "I don't think about it."

In his family, momentous dicta were given, but if one questioned them, the response was, "Forget it."

Mr. Spooner likened his family's reaction to questions to putting a cobra in the middle of the dining room table and being expected to eat as if nothing were unusual.

Mr. Spooner confronted his elderly mother about his sense of guilt over the death of his father. She said she had never told him she blamed him for his father's death. "You are too sensitive," she said. Her reaction did not surprise Mr. Spooner.

All the above incidents are fairly common situations in therapy. Sometimes, however, a therapist has a nagging feeling that the real issues are not surfacing. When that happens, I suspect denial about some sort of health fear. While sexual abuse is no longer a taboo topic, revelation of health fears seems to be. Sometimes that fear has as its basis a family history of illness. The expectation of illness carries a pall of doom with it.

To sweep away that pall requires that the therapist encourage clients to set future goals.

Ask your clients what they hope for. Initially help them set goals for therapy.

"What do you want to achieve in this hour?"

"How will you know if you achieve it?"

Help them make goals specific, not abstract. If they say, "I want to feel better," help them to determine what "feeling better" feels like.

"My hands will be sweat-free." "My mouth won't be dry." "My chest will feel quiet and untense."

Move from that session to their goals for the next week. "I will sing in the shower." "I will find something to laugh about once a day."

Check with them if they have met their goals. If they haven't, help them discover why they failed to achieve success.

If they have reached their goals, help clients analyze why success was possible.

After your client can set up one-week goals, help him or her set up three-month goals, six-month goals, and one-year goals. Setting goals and reaching them encourage people to believe in their power to achieve. It is a means to become a Fighter, rather than continuing life as a Fatalist.

"If I came from your family, I'd be very fearful. Of course, that's the way I'd feel. You might be braver than I am."

That was how I broached the expectation of heart disease to a man whose denial of fear was very strong.

An M.D. client who experienced physical symptoms when he was distressed in intimate relationships, learned to joke about them. He labelled them, "The seven plagues." Later, when a symptom would arise, he would laugh and accept it. As therapy progressed, the symptoms lasted a shorter and shorter time.

REWARDS OF ILLNESS

Ask clients to tell you what aspects of their illness are useful.

Therapists need to help clients recognize the value their illness has for them without making them feel guilty about having it. Asking them how they could gain the same rewards without being sick, if presented gently, can enable clients to discover how the same results might be obtained by means other than poor health.

A client learns that being sick in his or her family may be the only acceptable way to receive needed attention. In some families, the only way to avoid unpleasant chores, to attain notice, or to be unique is to be "the sickly one."

Anita, a participant in one of my illness seminars, told me she resolved not to be like her sickly sister. She watched her sister receive extra attention because she was "always sick." Anita, a fine artist, was rarely noticed.

As an adult, Anita would deny any physical problems because she couldn't abide the way her sister "manipulated everyone with her health problems."

Even when Anita was quite ill, she would not ask for attention because she was so fearful of being like her sister. Her husband and friends objected to her refusal to be tended to. Anita needed to discriminate between when it was appropriate to ask for help and when it wasn't.

She learned to ask herself when personal problems arose whether she would like to discuss the problem if a friend had it. If the answer was "Yes," Anita was to share the problem with her husband or friends.

Anita had no experience as a resource for healthy behavior. Her family had not taught her how to get attention apart from being sick. She has to create new ways that work.

Clients may accept that their accomplishments are minimal even when they are extraordinary. They don't expect any notice to be taken when they appear on a television show or when they visit a rock star's mansion.

They must decide how to get attention if they want it. Do they want attention for being funny? For being clever? For being compassionate?

How can they attain their goals?

It may be by hiring a publicist, by throwing a party, by getting an award.

The therapist can help enumerate ways, besides being sick, that clients can use for getting the attention they crave.

HEALTH CALENDAR AND ASSESSMENT

Urge clients who weren't taught how to get attention in their families of origin what methods they notice other people using to get attention. They will become aware that there are many other ways to get attention besides being sick. From that point, you can ask them if they see that the lifestyle they follow is a healthy one. If they tell you, "I follow healthy habits," have them be specific about what habits they follow.

Sometimes, people automatically follow healthy habits. They may find it easy to run, to avoid smoking, to eat a healthy diet. But they don't practice stress management. Filling out the Health Assessment in Chapter 6 will allow them to see where they need to improve.

For those clients who say, "I don't think about it," ask them to mark on a calendar when they have had a cold or other minor physical complaint. The dates of such maladies usually coincide with some major event in the family.

When clients say they are like one parent whose side of the family was healthy, the therapist can ask what causes them to reject the other parent. Often, resemblances to the rejected parent surface as a person grows older. Those resemblances may be physiological.

"Seeing is believing." Drawing a Genogram, a Life Drawing, or filling out a Health Assessment, a Health Calendar, or an

Energy Chart makes an impact that months of talking may not. Seeing the drawings may have an important impact on a client.

I sent a question to a group of head nurses to whom I was scheduled to give a workshop.

"Ask three patients what was going on in their families just before they entered the hospital."

By the time of the workshop, each of the head nurses was convinced of the influence of the family on the physical health of the patients.

THE COST OF ILLNESS TO THE FAMILY

Knowing what costs are of concern to clients may help a therapist to appreciate clients' fears more clearly. Harriet Hastings, a former client in her 60s, is a retired bank officer. She was widowed in her late 50s. With her husband's insurance, her pension fund, and Social Security, she lives a comfortable life.

However, whenever she is ill, she worries that she cannot afford the necessary medications prescribed.

Her health insurance does not include drug prescriptions. When she had a bout with influenza this past winter, she feared she could not afford the antibiotics to relieve severe stuffiness in her ears. She was afraid that without the drug she could endanger her hearing. Yet a 10-day supply cost $67.00, a major expenditure for her.

Harriet does not want her health needs to burden her grown children. So Harriet has taken a part-time job. In her work with me, paid for by her insurance, Harriet learned to share some of her concerns with her family.

Health insurance that pays nearly everything discourages one from taking responsibility for one's own health habits. It didn't reward Harriet for her daily swimming or her lack of overweight.

Some health insurance plans encourage a fatalistic attitude about health. They provide no incentive for being well through one's own initiative.

Mary Merit, the wife of the college professor we met in

Chapter 4, has invested in extra life insurance beyond that paid for by her husband's employer. She wanted to guard the family against the possibility of losing Bill as a breadwinner just at the time their son will be in college.

The additional coverage gives her some peace of mind about the future. She does not want their son's education to be at the mercy of his father's fatalism.

She practices as many preventive measures as she can so that her health will remain good.

"I think Bill, Jr. deserves to have at least one of us in good health."

INFORMATION

One way for therapists to show they personally believe in the future is to keep current with the most recent research on bodily treatment for illness, as well as with new mental health treatments.

Therapists need to know, for example, that the statistics of one in 10 women having breast cancer is true only after the age of 65 (Baker, 1991).

They need to know that the brother of a hemophiliac who does not himself have hemophilia is not a carrier of the disease. Sharing such information with clients, when pertinent, is necessary. So is encouraging clients to get physical exams when they feel sick.

It helps to tell clients when you, yourself, are receiving medical treatment. Observing your fighting attitude may be a new experience for them.

PERSONAL LIFESTYLE OF THERAPIST

The model of self-care the therapist gives clients is powerful. Consulting with a therapist who schedules clients until 2 a. m. and never takes a holiday had a strong negative influence on a client I saw. So, too, did a therapist who smoked. The client stopped therapy with him.

One of my former clients told me that she learned to treat herself to vacations after her work with me. I travel frequently and she learned to do that also. She was able to travel without feeling guilty.

I also let my clients know that I have frequent massage and that I walk every afternoon. As well as being a psychotherapist, I have an impact on my clients by my behavior. They learn from me what they failed to learn as a child.

This is especially so of women. They may have learned that they are lesser than men. Working with a woman therapist who believes in her own ability to accomplish things without having to follow someone else's script for her behavior allows them to emulate a woman who determines her own future.

THERAPISTS' CHECKLIST

Therapists should ask themselves questions about their own lifestyles.

Following are some suggested questions:

Medical Care

1. Do I fail to follow my physician's instructions—not take prescribed medicine, eat banned foods, fail to adhere to a weight loss plan? *no*
2. Do I notice body signals? *yes*
3. Do I tell myself the reason for memory loss, weakened vision or hearing, and poor balance is "I'm getting older"? NO
4. Do I carry health insurance? What does it include? *yes*
5. Does my medicine cabinet contain headache remedies, *some* laxatives, tranquilizers, weight-loss pills, and bandages?
6. Are there prescribed drugs in my medicine cabinet dated longer than six months ago? *yes*

7. Have I visited a psychotherapist for my own needs? *yes*
8. When I have a pain or body change that lasts for more than a week, do I consult a physician, chiropractor, or other health practitioner? *yes*
9. Do I ask my physician to recommend nonmedical treatments? *NO*
10. What kind of food do I eat? *Good + Bad*
11. How much sleep do I get per night? *8 hours*
12. Am I overweight by more than five percent? *?*

Stress Management

1. When I "see red," do I express my anger? *yes*
2. Do I practice meditation? *Sometimes*
3. Do I do things because I "have to"? *Sometimes*
4. Do I paint or play a musical instrument alone or with others? *NO*
6. Do I thank my friends or family for constructive criticism? *Sometimes*
7. Do I become angry when someone comments on my behavior? *NO*
8. Do I keep a journal, diary, or dream book? *NO*
9. What do I do for fun? How often? *Lots ·*

Work

1. Do I enjoy my work? *yes*
2. Is my work merely a means to make money? *No*
3. Do I feel there is no future in my job? *NO*
4. Do I like my co-workers or colleagues? *yes*
5. Does my boss appreciate me? *Yes*
6. Am I able to cancel a day's work because I need time off? *Yes* Do I wait until I am sick and cannot work before taking *no* time off? What are my secondary gains in being sick?
7. When I attend a conference, do I spend a good bit of my time making calls to clients and colleagues? *NO*

8. Do I wear a beeper? no
9. How many hours a week do I work? 35
10. Is there one issue besides my work that I feel passionate about? ?
11. If I were not a therapist, what would I be? ?
12. What about my co-workers? Is the only way they can have a spontaneous day off by being sick? NO
13. What is the major cause of clients' cancelling appointments?
14. What model do I give clients about taking time off? Do they see me in the office when I obviously need a vacation or am sick? NO
15. After clients have been sick, how do I react at their next appointment? Discuss

Family

1. Am I in contact with members of my family at least once a week? yes
2. Have I been in touch with every member of my family-of-origin within the last year? yes
3. When I am lonely or confused, do I call someone in my family for advice and support? yes
4. Do I turn to my family for financial help? NO
5. Does my extended family get together for casual events as well as for holidays, deaths, or weddings? yes
6. Do I know the birthdates—month, day and year—of my parents, brothers, and sisters? yes
7. Do I know my mother's maiden name and the maiden name of her mother? yes
8. If my parents, grandparents, or great-grandparents were immigrants, do I know the town they came from and where they first settled in America? NO
9. Do I think I will inherit the health pattern of my father's family? ? Probably not
10. Do I think I will inherit the health pattern of my mother's family? Hope not

Friends

1. Do I have a best friend? *No*
2. How often do I see him or her? *Not well*
3. What kinds of activities do I share with my friend?
4. Are my closest friends in my field of work? *No*
5. What topics do I fail to share with friends? *Everything*

Consider how reluctant or impatient you may have been to answer what is in your heart, not what you think is the right answer. In question #1 of Medical Care, for instance, have you always followed your doctor's orders? Did you really finish the medication even after you were feeling better? Maybe you can scan the answers and decide if there are any questions you want to change.

Consider the model you are presenting to your clients. Is it the model you want to present?

Are you living the lifestyle you want? Do you plan your future or does time simply vanish?

Helping clients confront their myths about health forces therapists to consider if they operate with the same myths their clients do.

Therapists have the advantage of meeting people who are open to learning. Usually, clients do not arrive at a therapist's office when all is well with them. Instead they appear because their lives are not satisfactory.

If the reason for the dissatisfaction proves to be the fear of inheriting poor health, as shown by a genogram and by the therapist's hunch that such is the case, the therapist might find some of the following methods helpful. There are ways to help clients design new health habits if they suffer from a legacy of expected illness:

1. Draw detailed genogram.
2. Have clients predict health future.
3. Receive specifics on what a client does for his or her good

health. Have him or her fill out a Health Assessment (Chapter 6).

4. Trust your own hunches. When therapy is drifting, consider physical fears as a possible subject your clients are not exposing.
5. Help clients design other ways to get attention besides being sick.
6. Have clients create a Life Drawing (Chapter 3).
7. Have clients make a Health Calendar that includes any illnesses that have occurred in the last six months.

Therapists need to complete a checklist on their own life-styles. What does it matter if therapists help their clients and fail to live long and healthy lives themselves?

ACTIVITIES

1. Ask yourself what will be your cause of death. Write it down and then assess what you are doing that will make your prediction come true.
2. Decide what one thing you can change of the things you are doing that are unhealthy. By when will you change that one thing?
3. Make reservations for your next two vacations.
4. How can you share more of yourself with friends or family?

APPENDIX A

HEALTH ASSESSMENT

I. Personal Choices

1. Do you visit the dentist at least once a year? Seeing a dentist for a check-up is an important way to make certain your mouth is in good health.
2. Do you use dental floss daily? Prevention is within your own hands.
3. Do you have your vision checked regularly? More people see their dentist regularly than see their eye doctor. But you have to determine how important your vision is to you.
4. Do you question your doctor about the necessity of the drugs he/she prescribes for you when you're ill? Do you simply take the medication prescribed? Or do you ask questions about the side effects or other information about the purpose of the medication?
5. Are you reluctant to use laxatives, tranquilizers, pain killers, reducing pills, and aspirin? Having faith that a healthy body can produce whatever it needs to stay healthy reduces the need to use synthetic means to substitute for a fully functional bodily system.
6. Have you ever asked your doctor for a nonmedical alternative?

It is useful to ask your doctor what was used in the days before antibiotics or cortisone to treat your current problem.

7. Have you ever disregarded the doctor's advice completely? The doctor as well as you yourself need to know that you consult experts to assist you in deciding on your own health. Sometimes that includes refusing to follow the doctor's advice, not because you disrespect the doctor but because you respect your inner wisdom.

8. Do you have health insurance? Health insurance routinely pays for tests when you are ill but not tests that are aimed at prevention.

9. Do you wear a seatbelt while riding in or driving a car? Some of the easiest things to do to be safe are the most neglected. A friend who works on the ambulance squad says that they never have to remove a seatbelt from a dead body. She notes that people without seatbelts are the only ones who die in automobile crashes.

10. Would you willingly visit a psychotherapist if it seemed indicated? Getting help for yourself when under undue stress or troubled by something in your past may be what would help you at a particular time in your life.

11. Do you keep a health journal? Memory of minor ailments such as a cold or the flu probably eludes you. Noting that you have a minor ailment at the same time each year may help you prepare for it the next year and keep you healthier.

II. Body Awareness

1. Do you have satisfactory sexual relationships? Sexual relationships that give you satisfaction are necessary to feeling self-esteem.

2. Are you pleased with the quality of your sexual relationships? Sexual relationships that you find demeaning do much to detract from your health.

3. Do you practice yoga or some form of stretching exercise at least 20 minutes three times or more a week? Finding what form of exercise pleases you is worth the investigation. Exercise that you enjoy will probably be easier to follow when you are feeling lazy or tired.

4. Do you jog or participate in some type of exercise at least three

times a week? The same applies here. An exercise you like is more likely to be followed when you are not as enthused about exercising.

5. Do you fall asleep easily at bedtime? Sometimes your mind is busily going over events of the day when you should be going to sleep. Learning stress management methods will help. So, too, will other things unique to your body. Those things may be having a cup of warm milk, taking a bath, reading something light, saying the rosary.

6. Do you feel rested when you awaken? Our bedroom faces East. When we get up, we see the sun rising too. Unless I feel rested, it is difficult to awaken with the excitement of the world's new day.

7. Is your weight within five percent of the ideal for your height? Sometimes people wait for a large weight gain before they decide to reduce the excess. However, if your pants seem snug or your skirt is tighter across your stomach, that is the time to heed your body's signals about your weight.

8. Do you have enough energy to accomplish your daily activities? You may have some physical malady or you may be feeling a mild depression. It is important to note how long the lack of energy remains. If it is fleeting, you probably won't have to do anything about it. If it continues for several weeks, check into it.

9. Do you feel at ease with your body? Comfort inside your own body requires you to know your body. It may be necessary to learn more about your body by having regular massage or by other means such as daily walks.

10. Do you breathe deeply and fully? Breathing shallowly does not fill your lungs with the oxygen that your organs need to function well.

11. Do you see an illness as an indication that something is out of balance in your lifestyle? Being annoyed at the development of an illness rather than seeing it as a message from yourself to yourself that something needs to be changed prompts you to eliminate the symptoms but not to discover what the underlying cause of the illness is.

12. When you are sick, do you find it easy to stop work, relax, and rest? You need to ask yourself if you could stop work, relax, and rest if you were not sick. Maybe you must be sick in order to give yourself permission to take it easy.

13. Do you refuse to smoke cigarettes? Since everyone now knows

that cigarette smoking is bad for health, does your continuing to smoke mean something else to you? Do you feel that you won't live a long life anyway or that to show fear of something external is not manly?

III. Stress and Stress Management

1. Do you engage in any creative activities, either alone or with a group? Playing chamber music or painting a mural with other people or by yourself plumbs the inner creative forces that calm your feelings and promote self-awareness.
2. Do you feel it is O.K. to get angry or say "No" to someone? After being angry with someone do you then feel comfortable or are you still seething several hours or days later? You may have to learn that anger is an appropriate feeling and that it does not mean you are a bad person.
3. Are you able to resolve conflict when it occurs? Resolving conflict at the moment it happens rather than allowing your body to be a storehouse of troubled feelings for a length of time keeps your body healthy.
4. Are you able to recognize when worry and anxiety increase to the point of interfering with your lifestyle? If you ruminate about a situation so that you cannot focus on anything else, you are allowing worry and anxiety to control your life.
5. Do you feel that the best way to deal with strong emotional feelings is to confront them? When you have strong emotional feelings, positive or negative, it is helpful to confront them. Maybe you are uncomfortable expressing feelings of love to a friend. Or you might have more trouble with the negative feelings. Try to show your love by a simple act. It may be delivering a bouquet from your garden to the person you feel love towards. It may be visualizing your difficult boss as a five-year-old child.
6. Do you regularly reduce stress by setting aside a time for yourself to use a specific relaxation technique? When you are busy, you may tell yourself you have no time to practice relaxation techniques. That is the precise time you need to make yourself a priority.
7. Do you use massage or some other type of "hands on" method for relaxation? Scheduling massage regularly will force you to take time for yourself.

8. Do you set aside at least one hour each day for "play," that is, some activity that is done for enjoyment only? Write up a few pages of play activities. They may be time spent in the garden, playing tennis, tap dancing. Put on your list any activities you find enjoyable. Whatever mood you are in, there will be an activity that coincides with your feelings of the moment. Be sure to practice one of the activities at least an hour each day.

IV. Environmental Awareness

1. Do you make use of transportation other than automobiles when possible? Walking, running, skating, biking, canoeing, rowing, horseback riding, swimming are all forms of transportation that require using your body. Be sure to use some of them as often as possible.
2. Do you keep your thermostat at 65 or lower in the winter? Having your house or office really warm does not motivate you to exercise to warm up your blood. While keeping your thermostat lower saves fuel, it also forces you to use your own fuel-making apparatus.
3. Do you use nonpolluting and nontoxic cleaning agents and avoid exposure to chemicals, sprays, and exhaust fumes? Being conscious of the toxins in the atmosphere stimulates man's consciousness about the toxins he introduces into his own personal environment.

V. Nutritional Awareness

1. Do you eat your meals in a quiet relaxed environment? You can eat your meals with lighted candles and flowers on the table or you can eat in front of the television set. Watching mayhem while you eat does not help to keep you in a stress-free environment. You can control the setting for refueling your body.
2. Do you eat at least one uncooked fruit or vegetable per day? Plan to make your snacks something that is healthful to your body.
3. Do you limit the use of coffee and non-herbal teas to three cups per day? Being energized by the use of caffeine allows your body to stop creating its own energy.

4. Do you read labels carefully to check for food additives? At least once a month, you can spend extra time in the food market reading labels. You do not always have time for such carefulness, so plan it once a month. Then you can buy the products you have checked on.

5. Do you eat well-balanced meals selected from the four basic food groups? You may have grown up in a home where there was a preponderance of foods that always were eaten by the family. Maybe those foods were the cheapest and most filling for an immigrant family. You can change that now. Use the traditional family recipes for special occasions. You don't have to give up ever having them. Just save their use for occasional times.

6. Are you aware of your own nutritional needs and how to meet them? Perhaps you must add more calcium to your diet or more of the B vitamins. You can find out about your personal nutritional needs and then make sure your diet supplies them.

7. Do you limit the consumption of alcohol to minimal amounts? It is not necessary to discontinue totally the use of alcohol, but moderating its use provides a healthier body. Some studies indicate that having a drink a day is helpful to the heart. No studies I know of indicate that becoming mildly intoxicated is a useful aid to any of the bodily functions.

Appendix B

FAMILY ILLNESSES: SOURCES OF INFORMATION

There are, of course, illnesses that surface in families because of genetic factors. These include Tay-Sachs, Sickle Cell Anemia, Retinoblastoma, Hyperlipidemia, Hodgkinson's Chorea, Cystic Fibrosis. Even with those, however, not all the children in an affected family inevitably develop the illness. Family members are "at risk" to develop the illness, but do not necessarily develop it.

Take Tay-Sachs, for example. It is not true that both parents have to descend from Ashkenazi Jews, since all population groups can carry the gene for Tay-Sachs. However, both parents must be Tay-Sachs carriers. If they are, then each child they conceive has a 25 percent chance of having the illness and a 50 percent chance of also being a carrier. Fewer than 20 children are born in the United States with Tay-Sachs each year. Sickle-Cell Anemia is similar to Tay-Sachs. Both parents must be carriers of the trait in order for their children to be at-risk to develop the illness. About one in every 1000 African-Americans has Sickle Cell Anemia.

Retinoblastoma is an illness that can cause blindness in babies. It is necessary that women coming from families with the disease or whose husbands come from such families tell

179

their obstetricians of the possibility of their children developing the illness. Some 75 percent of those having retinoblastoma do not come from families affected by the disease. The earlier the treatment, the less the likelihood of total blindness. Another illness that runs in families is hyperlipidemia, one of the heart diseases that can be diagnosed early in a child's life. Such a diagnosis means that a person's levels of low-density lipoprotein (LDL) cholesterol is unusually high because the body's DNA repair mechanisms cannot break down LDL cholesterol.

When illnesses do run in your family, receiving genetic counselling is necessary. Such counselors will map your family health history and may advise some medical tests. Sources of such counselling can be obtained through your local medical society or the National Society of Genetic Counselors, Inc.

Educating oneself about an illness is uncommon. You expect the physician, his or her nurses, and the ancillary caretakers to know about an illness they are treating you for. But they and you do not expect you to know as much about the malady as you can.

Does it make sense to know how your computer works or how heat is conducted in your kitchen pots and not know how cancer spreads or hearts deteriorate? An endocrinologist once told me not to listen to any information about thyroids when I asked her a question about mine. I found a new endocrinologist who was happy to answer my questions (see Chapter 7 on choosing a physician). Learn as much about the family illness as possible.

Since certain illnesses were unnamed some years ago, you may not have appropriate warning since the family may not know about its risk. However, if you learn that there were a number of early deaths (before 55) in the family, you can suspect there is a familial illness at work. You may discover that all early deaths were in members of the same sex. Or that the same area of the body was involved. If you are planning to have children, discover if there is treatment before the baby is born to eliminate the possibility of inheriting the family illness. If that is not viable, discover if early treatment makes the later symptoms less likely.

Be certain to contact the Alliance of Genetic Support Groups,

1001 22nd St. N.W., Suite 800, Washington, D.C. 20037 for information and monthly newsletters. Call 1-800-336-GENE.

Also contact the National Society of Genetic Counselors, Inc. at 223 Canterbury Drive, Wallingford, Pa. 19086 for information on what Genetic Counseling is, but not about specific genetic disabilities.

The National Center for Education in Maternal and Child Health at 38th & R Streets, N.W. Washington, D.C. 20057, 202-625-8400 has published a directory of known national genetic voluntary organizations. Their guide is available for the asking. Some organizations they include follow:

General

March of Dimes Birth Defects Foundation
1275 Mamaroneck Ave.
White Plains, NY 10605

National Easter Seal Society
2033 W. Ogden Ave.
Chicago, IL 60612

National Foundation for Jewish Genetic Diseases, Inc.
250 Park Ave.
Suite 1000
New York, NY 10177

National Organization for Rare Disorders, Inc.
P.O. Box 8923
New Fairfield, CT 06812

Sibling Information Network
University Affiliated Program on Developmental Disabilities
University of Connecticut
249 Glenbrook Rd.
Box U-64
Storrs, CT 06268

TASH: The Assn. for Persons with Severe Handicaps
7010 Roosevelt Way, N. E.
Seattle, WA 98115

Auditory

Alexander Graham Bell Assn. for the Deaf
3417 Volta Place, N. W.
Washington, D. C. 20007

American Society for Deaf Children
814 Thayer Ave.
Silver Spring, MD 20910

Cancer

American Cancer Society, Inc.
3340 Peachtree Rd., N. E.
Atlanta, GA 30026

Candlelighters Childhood Cancer Foundation
1901 Pennsylvania Ave., N. W.
Suite 1011
Washington, D. C. 20006

Family Polyposis Registry
Toronto General Hospital
200 Elizabeth St.
Eaton Bldg. 10-315
Toronto, Ontario MFG 2C4
Canada

**Intestinal Multiple Polyposis and
 Colorectal Cancer**
1006-1001 Brinker Dr.
Hagerstown, MD 21740

Leukemia Society of America, Inc.
733 Third Ave.
New York, NY 10017

National Cancer Care Foundation
1180 Ave. of the Americas
New York, NY 10036

Cardiovascular

**Council on Cardiovascular Disease
 in the Young**
**American Heart Assn. National
 Center**
7320 Greenville Ave.
Dallas, TX 75231

Chromosomal

**Assn. for Children with Down's
 Syndrome, Inc.**
2616 Martin Ave.
Bellmore, Long Island, NY 11710

Fragile X Foundation
P. O. Box 300233
Denver, CO 80203

National Assn. for Down's Syndrome
P. O. Box 4542
Oak Brook, IL 60521

Prader-Willi Syndrome Assn.
6490 Excelsior Blvd.
E-102
St. Louis Park, MN

Turner's Syndrome Society
York University
Administrative Studies
Building #006
4700 Keele St.
Downsview, Ontario M3J 1P3
Canada

Connective Tissue

National Marfan Foundation
382 Main St.
Port Washington, NY 11050

Craniofacial

American Cleft Palate Assn.
1218 Grandview Ave.
University of Pittsburgh
Pittsburgh, PA 15211

Developmental Disabilities

**Assn. for Children and Adults with
 Learning Disabilities, Inc.**
4156 Library Rd.
Pittsburgh, PA 15234

Autism Society of America
1234 Massachusetts Ave., N. W.
Suite 1017
Washington, D. C. 20005-4599

**Center for Hyperactive Child
 Information, Inc.**
P. O. Box 66272
Washington, D. C. 20035-6272

Orton Dyslexia Society
724 York Rd.
Baltimore, MD 21204

United Cerebral Palsy Associations, Inc.
66 East 34th St.
New York, NY 10016

Gastrointestinal

American Celiac Society
45 Gifford Ave.
Jersey City, NJ 07304

American Liver Foundation
998 Pompton Ave.
Cedar Grove, NJ 07009

Gluten Intolerance Group of North America
P. O. Box 23055
Seattle, WA 98102-0353

National Foundation for Ileitis and Colitis, Inc.
44 Park Ave.
New York, NY 10016-7374

Hematologic

Cooley's Anemia Foundation,Inc.
105 E. 22nd St.
Suite 911
New York, NY 10010

Iron Overload Diseases Assn., Inc.
224 Datura St.
Suite 311
W. Palm Beach, FL 33401

National Assn. for Sickle Cell Disease, Inc.
4221 Wilshire Blvd.
Suite 360
Los Angeles, CA 90010-3503

National Hemophilia Foundation
The Soho Bldg.
110 Greene St.
Room 406
New York, NY 10012

Immunologic

American Lupus Society
23751 Madison St.
Torrance, CA 90505

Immune Deficiency Foundation
P. O. Box 586
Columbia, MD 21045

Lupus Foundation of America, Inc.
1717 Massachusetts Ave., N. W.
Suite 203
Washington, D. C. 20036

Sjogen's Syndrome Foundation, Inc.
29 Gateway Dr.
Great Neck, NY 11021

Kidney

National Kidney Foundation, Inc.
2 Park Ave.
New York, NY 10016

Metabolic

American Diabetes Assn., Inc.
1660 Duke St.
Alexandria, VA 22314

American Porphyria Foundation
P. O. Box 11163
Montgomery, AL 36111

Assn. for Gycogen Storage Disease
Box 896
Durant, IA 52747

Assn. of Neuro-Metabolic Disorders
5223 Brookfield Lane
Sylvania, OH 43560

Cystic Fibrosis Foundation
6931 Arlington Rd.
Bethesda, MD 20814

Dysautonomia Foundation, Inc.
370 Lexington Ave.
New York, NY 10017

**Foundation for the Study of Wilson's
Disease, Inc.**
5447 Palisade Ave.
Bronx, NY 10471

Lowe's Syndrome Assn., Inc.
222 Lincoln St.
West Lafayette, IN 47906

**Malignant Hyperthermia Assn. of
the United States**
P. O. Box 3231
Darien, CT 06320

**Maple Syrup Urine Disease Family
Support Group**
R.R. #2
Box 24-A
Flemingsburg, KY 41041

ML (Mucolipidosis) IV Foundation
6 Concord Dr.
Monsey, NY 10952

National Gaucher Foundation, Inc.
1424 K St., N. W.
Washington, D. C. 20005

**National Mucopolysaccharidoses
Society, Inc.**
17 Kraemer St.
Hicksville, NY 11801

**National Organization for Albinism
and Hypopigmentation**
1500 Locust St.
Suite 1811
Philadelphia, PA 19102-4316

**National Tay-Sachs and Allied
Diseases Assn., Inc.**
385 Elliot St.
Newton, MA 02164

Organic Acidemia Assn., Inc.
1532 South 87th St.
Kansas City, Kansas 66111

**United Leukodystrophy Foundation,
Inc.**
2304 Highland Dr.
Sycamore, IL 60178

Williams Syndrome Assn.
P. O. Box 178373
San Diego, CA 92117-0910

Wilson's Disease Assn.
P. O. Box 75324
Washington, D. C. 20013

**Zain Hansen M.P.S. Foundation
Mucopolysacharridoses**
P. O. Box 4768
1200 Fernwood Dr.
Arcata, CA 95521

Musculoskeletal

**Arthritis Foundation/American
Juvenile Arthritis Organization**
1314 Spring St., N. W.
Atlanta, GA 30309

**Freeman-Sheldon Parent Support
Group**
1459 East Maple Hills Dr.
Bountiful, Ut 84010

National Scoliosis Foundation, Inc.
93 Concord Ave.
P. O. Box 547
Belmont, MA 02178

**Osteogenesis Imperfecta
Foundation, Inc.**
P. O. Box 14807
Tampa, FL 34629-4807

Scoliosis Assn., Inc.
P. O. Box 51353
Raleigh, N. C. 27609

Neurologic

**Alzheimer's Disease and Related
Disorders Assn., Inc.**
70 East Lake St.
Chicago, IL 60601

American Narcolepsy Assn.
P. O. Box 1187
San Carlos, CA 94070

American Parkinson Disease Assn.
116 John St.
Suite 417
New York, NY 10038

**Batten's Disease Support and
Research Assn.**
6707 197th St, E.
Spanaway, WA 98387

Epilepsy Foundation of America
4351 Garden City Dr.
Landover, MD 20785

**Friedreich's Ataxia Group in
America, Inc.**
P. O. Box 11116
Oakland, CA 94611

Hereditary Disease Foundation
606 Wilshire Blvd.
Suite 504
Santa Monica, CA 90401-9990

**Huntingdon's Disease Society of
America, Inc.**
140 W. 22nd St.
New York, NY 10011-2420

**International Joseph Diseases
Foundation, Inc.**
P. O. Box 2550
Livermore, CA 94550

National Hydrocephalus Foundation
Route 1
River Rd. Box 210A
Joliet, IL 60436

**National Neurofibromatosis
Foundation, Inc.**
141 Fifth Ave.
Suite 7-S
New York, NY 10010

National Parkinson Foundation, Inc.
1501 Northwest 9th Ave.
Bob Hope Rd.
Miami, FL 33136-1494

**National Spasmodic Torticollis
Assn.**
P. O. Box 873
Royal Oak, MI 48068-0873

**National Tuberous Sclerosis Assn.,
Inc.**
4351 Garden City Dr.
Suite 660
Landover, MD 20785

Parkinson's Disease Foundation, Inc.
650 W. 168th St.
New York, NY 10032-9982

Parkinson's Educational Program USA
1800 Park Newport
#302
Newport Beach, CA 92660

Reflex Sympathetic Dystrophy Syndrome Assn.
822 Wayside Lane
Haddonfield, NJ 08033

Spina Bifida Assn. of America
1700 Rockville Pike
Suite 540
Rockville, MD 20852

Sturge-Weber Foundation
P. O. Box 460931
Aurora, CO 80015

Tourette Syndrome Assn., Inc.
42-40 Bell Blvd.
Bayside, NY 11361

Tuberous Sclerosis Assn. of America, Inc.
P. O. Box 1305
Middleboro, MA 02370

Families of Spinal Muscular Atrophy
P. O. Box 1465
Highland Park, IL 60035

Muscular Dystrophy Assn.
810 Seventh Ave.
New York, NY 10019

Myasthenia Gravis Foundation Inc.
7-11 South Broadway
Suite 304
White Plains, NY 10601

Myoclonus Families United
1564 East 34th St.
Brooklyn, NY 11234

National Ataxia Foundation
600 Twelve Oaks Center
15500 Wayzata Blvd.
Wayzata, MN 55391

National Multiple Sclerosis Society
205 E. 42nd St.
New York, NY 10017

Neuromuscular

Amyotrophic Lateral Sclerosis Assn., Inc.
15300 Ventura Blvd.
Suite 315
Sherman Oaks, CA 91403

Charcot-Marie-Tooth International, Inc.
34 Bayview Dr.
St. Catherines, Ontario L2N 4Y6
Canada

Short Stature

Human Growth Foundation
4720 Montgomery Lane
Bethesda, MD 20815

Little People of America, Inc.
P. O. Box 633
San Bruno, CA 94066

Skin

**Dystrophic Epidermolysis Bullosa
Research Assn. of America, Inc.**
Kings County Medical Center
451 Clarkson Ave.
Bldg. E-6-101, Sixth Floor
Brooklyn, NY 11203

**National Congenital Port Wine Stain
Foundation**
125 East 63rd St.
New York, NY 10021

**National Foundation for Ectodermal
Dysplasias**
108 North First St.
Suite 311
Mascoutah, IL 62258

**United Scleroderma Foundation,
Inc.**
P. O. Box 350
Watsonville, CA 95077-0350

Visual

**American Foundation for the Blind,
Inc.**
15 W. 16th St.
New York, NY 10011

Assn. for Macular Diseases, Inc.
210 E. 64th St.
New York, NY 10021

**National Assn. for Parents of the
Visually Impaired, Inc.**
P. O. Box 180806
Austin, TX 78718

**National Assn. for Visually
Handicapped**
22 West 21st St. 6th Floor
New York, NY 10010

SUPPORT GROUPS

There are also support groups for many illnesses. Your local hospital can help you find support groups, as can the following:

Alliance of Genetic Support Groups
38th and R Streets, N. W.
Washington, D. C. 20057

The National Center for Education in Maternal and Child Health, 38th and R Streets, N. W., Washington, D. C. 20057 will send you on request a free booklet on starting self-help groups.

It would trivialize hereditary illness to minimize its impact on those who live in its shadow. It is true that statistics assert that only 50 percent of children of parents who both are carriers of a defective gene will develop some "family" illnesses. Yet if you are a person in such a family, you may worry that you will fall in the unhealthy 50 percent. And in fact, you may.

Your greatest protection is being familiar with current research about the "family illness."

Appendix C

THERAPISTS' CHECKLIST

Being a therapist promotes certain problems. Chief among them is burnout. I don't think burnout derives from listening to a person's problems, but rather from assuming that one has to be perfect.

Clergymen and women are entitled to listen and then pray with the seeker of solace. Therapists are not entitled to use the same method. They expect themselves to provide answers that will help their clients. Clients have the same expectation.

The checklist provided in Chapter 9 asks questions in five areas of a therapist's life—Medical Care, Stress Management, Work, Family, and Friends. This Appendix analyzes each answer separately. Compare your answers with the expansion of each.

Medical Care

1. Do I fail to follow my physician's instructions, not take prescribed medicine, eat banned foods, fail to adhere to a weight loss plan?

   Maybe you don't really trust that physician. Is it time you looked for another instead of ignoring this one's advice? You may need to consult a therapist about continually failing to lose weight.

189

2. Do I notice body signals?

   Your body signals you by being tired when you awaken, having frequent chest pains or suffering regular headaches. Respect for such signals is imperative.

3. Do I tell myself the reason for memory loss, weakened vision or hearing, and poor balance is "I'm getting older"?

   "I'm getting older" may be true but your symptoms may have nothing to do with being older. Check them out first.

4. Do I carry health insurance? What does it include?

   Does your health insurance reimburse you for illness but not for prevention?

5. Does my medicine cabinet contain headache remedies, laxatives, tranquilizers, weight loss pills, and bandages?

   Look into your medicine chest. It will help you recognize what issues you are always prepared for or fear. Do you always have headache remedies on hand?

6. Are there prescribed drugs in my medicine cabinet dated longer than six months ago?

   Do you keep old medications long after you have recovered good health? You may be expecting to have that illness again. You are preparing for it.

7. Have I visited a psychotherapist for my own needs?

   Do you still believe that only crazy people visit therapists?

8. When I have a pain or body change that lasts for more than a week, do I consult a physician, chiropractor, or other health practitioner?

   Are you overly patient about persistent bodily signals?

9. Do I ask my physician to recommend nonmedical treatments?

   Because I am very sensitive to antibiotics, I ask my physician for the old remedies.

10. What kind of food do I eat?

    Being aware of what fuels your body is certainly as important as filling your car's engine with appropriate fuel. You don't use regular gas in a car that requires diesel fuel. Eating a diet rich in fat, sugar, red meat encourages heart and other problems.

11. How much sleep do I get per night?

    Regular sleep does much to counterbalance stress. If you have a sleep problem (over two weeks of troubled sleep patterns), use methods to overcome it. Those methods include having a regular sleep time, not eating after dinner, being warm or cool enough, using bed only for sleep or sex, getting up if you cannot sleep for over half an hour.

12. Am I overweight by more than five percent?

If your weight is five percent over the ideal weight for you as shown in insurance tables, start losing the extra pounds right away. Waiting until it is 10 percent or more makes the job harder, the time devoted to weight loss longer, and the impact on your body more serious. Put the light out in the kitchen and make it off limits after dinnertime.

Stress Management

1. When I "see red," do I express my anger?

Expressing anger does not require a scene worthy of an Academy Award. It may simply mean saying in a mild tone of voice, "I won't tolerate that kind of behavior." Swallowing anger appears to resurface in maladies.

2. Do I practice meditation?

There are many varieties of meditation. Find out which works best for you. I meditate best in the tub, sitting in water.

3. Do I do things because I "have to"?

Drawing a wheel that divides how you spend your day allows you to recognize whether or not any of your activities are done for fun only.

4. Do I paint or play a musical instrument alone or with others?

Leaving some time for creativity alone or with friends refreshes your spirit.

5. Do I thank my friends or family for constructive criticism?

Amrit Desai (1990), a yogi, says, "Be thankful for anyone who shows you your faults. You cannot see them alone."

6. Do I become angry when someone comments on my behavior?

Reacting to criticism by resenting it does not encourage your friends or family to point out negative behavior. Being surrounded by "yesmen" does not assure you of growth.

7. Do I keep a journal, diary, or dream book?

Keeping an account of your feelings or your dreams keeps you aware of yourself.

8. What do I do for fun? How often?

Each day should contain some fun. Setting aside an hour for fun requires commitment to self.

Fun for one person–gardening, for example–may be hard work for someone else. What is fun for you? Write a list of things that are fun for you (See Chapter 8).

Work

1. Do I enjoy my work?

   When you awaken, are you eager to get to work? How much healing are you getting out of your work? Work requires you to believe you are paying your rent to live on Earth. Even the most mundane work is needed by others. However, if you don't feel that way, you shouldn't continue in the work you are doing.

2. Is my work merely a means to make money?

   If so, you can ask yourself if there is any other way you can make money. If there isn't, you need to discover how you can make this job good for you. What might you need to learn from this situation?

3. Do I feel there is no future in my job?

   You need to ask yourself if you want a job with a future. You might be satisfied doing what you are currently doing.

4. Do I like my co-workers or colleagues?

   If you like your co-workers, you may tolerate other features of the job that are unsatisfactory. You might ask yourself if you stay with the job simply because the other people you work with make work tolerable. Better jobs may also hire nice people.

5. Does my boss appreciate me?

   When you do a good job, does your boss say so? If not, you can make it apparent that you are doing good work. For example, you can make a poster that shows the work of your department in color. Then hang it over your desk. You can join an organization that brings together people in your field. You can reward yourself when you accomplish something—put fresh flowers on your desk, for example.

6. What are my secondary gains in being sick? Am I able to cancel a day's work because I need time off? Do I wait until I am sick and cannot work before taking time off?

   If the only time you take off from work is when you are sick, being sick has some reward. Maybe you need to take off for reasons other than sickness.

7. When I attend a conference, do I spend a good bit of my time making calls to clients?

Even when your job sends you to a conference, you may fill up relaxation time with making telephone calls to clients. You deserve some time away from work. Your company thought so, too, or they wouldn't have sent you away.

8. Do I wear a beeper?

Sometimes, work requires that you wear a beeper. Other times, you may wear one to convince yourself that you are important. It also keeps you from ever really "being here now." You are always "on call," thus basically unavailable to the person you're with at the moment.

9. How many hours a week do I work?

In the 90s, being at work less is becoming the rage. Some people who spent 60-80 hours at work are asking themselves, "What for?" If work is the only place you feel "at home," you need to ask yourself what other situations would provide the comfort you get at work.

10. Is there one issue besides my work that I feel passionate about?

Feeling passionate about snake farms is better than not feeling passionate about anything. Put some passion in your life.

11. If I were not a therapist, what would I be?

Being a therapist allows one to feel the pulse of life, but it is someone else's life. Being an expert at something else you could make a living from is necessary.

12. What about my co-workers? Can they have a spontaneous day off only by being sick?

Co-workers who take off only if they are sick have an effect on us.

13. What is the major cause of clients' cancelling appointments?

Clients cancelling appointments for reasons of health reflect back to you what they learn from you. Sickness is an excuse to postpone life.

14. What model do I give clients about taking time off? Do they see me in the office when I obviously need time off?

Clients often model themselves after behavior they note in their therapists. If they see you in the office when you need time off, what does that tell them? What does it tell you?

15. After clients have been sick, how do I react at their next appointment?

Spending a lot of time discussing illness and treatments for illness gives the message to clients that being sick takes precedence over any other life events.

Family

1. Am I in contact with members of my family at least once a week?

   The most natural support system is the family. My Aunt Mary, besides being very nurturing to me, was also the one who could tell me I was "getting fleshy."
2. Have I been in touch with every member of my family-of-origin within the last year?

   Call or write notes to members of your family-of-origin or send photographs of close relatives who may no longer be alive except in memory.
3. When I am lonely or confused, do I call someone in my family for advice and support?

   Asking advice and support from relatives who know you can be helpful. They usually love you unconditionally. With them you have no image to uphold. Even when you're being a jerk, they accept you.
4. Do I turn to my family for financial help?

   Maybe a cousin would be your best source for a loan.
5. Does my extended family get together for casual events as well as for holidays, deaths, or weddings?

   Begin to initiate family gatherings for minor events. Stop saying "I only see you when someone dies."
6. Do I know the birthdates, month, day and year, of my parents, brothers, and sisters?

   Make it your business to know the complete birthdate of family members.
7. Do I know my mother's maiden name and the maiden name of her mother?

   How much information about your family do you know?
8. If my parents, grandparents or great-grandparents were immigrants, do I know the town they came from and where they first settled in America?

   Knowing immigrant information allows you to feel more rooted to a family. Find out why your family settled where they did. It may have been that other villagers moved to that spot or that the ship's captain was paid off to deliver immigrants to Boston. Even though your forebears planned on going to New York, they may have wound up in New England.

9. Do I think I will inherit the health pattern of my father's family?

Believing you will inherit a terminal family illness along with your blue eyes may rest like a cloud over your life. You need to learn as much as you can about the illness and its current treatment. Is there a test that can be done to discover if you will inherit the illness? See the addresses of national genetic counseling centers in Appendix B.

10. Do I think I will inherit the health pattern of my mother's family?

Gynecologists routinely ask if your sister or mother had breast cancer. Research shows that only 20 percent of women who develop breast cancer came from families having cancer (Gross & Ito, 1990).

Friends

1. Do I have a best friend?

Having a best friend to talk to about anything has a positive impact on one's life.

2. How often do I see him or her?

Having a best friend and seeing or talking to him or her frequently is helpful. One of my clients spoke of having a best friend several hundred miles away. The friendship was waning because the wives didn't have the bond the husbands did. My client learned to see his friend alone once a year and to call him every couple of weeks.

3. What kinds of activities do I share with my friend?

A close friend may be someone you can share puns with or shop with or go to the races with.

4. Are my closest friends in my field of work?

You may want friends who are also therapists and understand the stresses of your work.

5. What topics do I fail to share with friends?

Do you believe that if your friends knew how you feel about certain topics they would no longer care for you? Whenever you talk to them, do you edit your speech?

Bibliography

Bailer, John. In *American Health*, March, 1989, p. 14.

Baker, Nancy C. *Relative Risk*, New York: Penguin, 1991.

Bannerman, Catherine. The genogram and elderly patients. *The Journal of Family Practice*, Vol. 235, 1986, pp. 426–428.

Benson, Herbert. *Beyond the Relaxation Response*. New York: Times Books, 1984.

Bishop, Anne H. and Scudder, John R. *Caring, Curing, Coping: Nurse, Physician, Patient Relationship. Tuscaloosa, Alabama:* Univ. of Alabama Press, 1985.

Blake, Peggy and Frye, Robert. *Discover Your Health Behaviors, A Self-Assessment & Behavior Change Manual*. New York: Random House, 1988.

Borysenko, Joan. *Guilt Is the Teacher, Love Is the Lesson*. New York: Warner Books, 1990.

Cannon, Walter B. "Voodoo" death. *American Anthropologist*, April-June 1942.

Cassell, Eric J. *Talking with Patients*, Vols. 1 & 2. Cambridge, Mass.: MIT Press, 1985.

Chopra, Deepak. *Creating Health*. New York: Houghton Mifflin, 1987.

Chopra, Deepak. *Quantum Healing*. New York: Bantam, 1989.

Conger, Beach. *Bag Balm & Duct Tape Tales of a Vermont Doctor.* Boston: Little, Brown, 1988.

Cousins, Norman. *Anatomy of an Illness*. New York: W. W. Norton, 1979.

Cousins, Norman. *Head First: The Biology of Hope.* New York: E. P. Dutton, 1989.

Cousins, Norman, *Omni,* vol. 12, December 1989.

Crispell, Kenneth R. and Gomez, Carlos F. *Hidden Illness in the White House.* Durham, North Carolina: Duke University Press, 1988.

Davis, Natalie. *Heartbeat: The Politics of Health Research.* Springer, New York, 1976.

Desai, Amrit. *Reflections.* Lenox, Mass: Kripalu Center, 1990.

Dossey, Larry. *Space, Time and Medicine.* Boston: Shambhala Publications, 1982.

Dundy, Elaine. *Elvis & Gladys.* New York: Macmillan,1985.

Emery, Alan E. H. *Genetic Engineering.* Berkeley: University of California Press, 1968.

Epstein, Gerald. *Healing Visualizations: Creating Health Through Imagery.* New York: Bantam Books, 1989.

Feste, Catherine. *The Physician Within: Taking Charge of Your Well-Being.* Minnetonka, MN: Diabetes Center, 1987.

Frankel, Richard M., Morse, Diane S., Suchman, Anthony and Beckman, Howard B., Can I really improve my listening skills with only 15 minutes to see my patients? *HMO Practice,* Vol. 5, No. 4, 1991.

Garrett, Robert E., Klinkman, Michael and Post, Linda. If you meet Buddha on the road, take a genogram: Zen and the art of family medicine. *Family Medicine,* Vol. 19 No. 3, 1987.

Gerson, Randy and McGoldrick, Monica. The Computerized Genogram. *Primary Care,* Vol. 12, No. 3, Sept. 1, 1985, pp. 535–545.

Goldwyn, Robert M. *The Patient and the Plastic Surgeon.* Boston: Little Brown, 1981.

Gormley, Myra Vanderpool. *Family Diseases: Are You At Risk?,* Baltimore: Geneological Publishing Co., 1989.

Grayzel, Solomon. *A History of the Jews.* Philadelphia: The Jewish Publication Society of America, 1947.

Green, Lawrence W. The trade-off between the expediency of health promotion and the durability of health education. In: Ed. Stan Maes, et. al. *Topics in Health Psychology.* New York: John Wiley & Sons, Ltd., 1988.

Gross, Amy and Ito, Dee. *Women Talk about Breast Surgery.* New York: Crown, 1990.

Hall, Robert J., Elayda, MacArthur, A., Gray, Albert, et al., CAB: Long term folow-up of 22, 284 consecutive patients. *Circulation Part II*, 63 (3), Sept. 1983.

Harsanyi, Zsolt and Hutton, Richard. *Genetic Prophecy: Beyond the Double Helix*. New York: Rawson, Wade, 1981.

Hendin, David and Marks, Joan. *The Genetic Connection*. New York: Wm. Morrow & Co., 1978.

Hutschnecker, Arnold. *The Will to Live*. New York: Cornerstone Library, 1978.

Jones, J. Alfred and Phillips, Gerald M. *Communicating with Your Doctor: Rx for Good Medical Care*. Carbondale Il: Southern Illinois University Press, 1988.

Justice, Blair. *Who Gets Sick?* Houston: Peak Press, 1987.

Karpman, Stephen. Script drama analysis. *Transactional Analysis Bulletin*, 1968, p. 39–43.

Killip, T. Coronary artery surgery study, a randomized trial of coronary bypass surgery: Eight years of follow-up and survival in patients with reduced ejection fraction. *Circulation*, 1985 No. 116, pp. 102–110.

Kirsta, Alix. *The Book of Stress Survival*. New York: Simon & Schuster, 1986.

Klieman, Charles and Osborn, Kevin. *Heart Disease*. New York: Bantam, 1991.

Landon, Michael. LIFE Magazine, June, 1991.

LeShan, Lawrence. *How to Meditate*. New York: Bantam Books, 1973.

Levine, Stephen. *Who Dies?* Garden City, NY: Anchor Books, 1982.

Lynch, James. *The Broken Heart*. New York: Basic Books, 1977.

Mantle, Mickey. *The Mick*. New York: Doubleday, 1985.

Mauer, Janet R. *How to Talk to Your Doctor: Getting Beyond the Medical Mystique*. New York: Simon & Schuster, 1986.

McGoldrick, Monica and Gerson, Randy. *Genograms in Family Assessment*. New York: W. W. Norton, 1985.

McKusick, Victor. *Mendelian Inheritance in Man*. Baltimore: The Johns Hopkins U. Press, 1988.

Michener, James. Living with an ailing heart. *New York Times Magazine*, August 19, 1984.

Milunsky, Aubrey. *Choices, Not Chances*. Boston: Little, Brown, 1977.

Moss, Ralph W. *Unraveling the Politics*. New York: Paragon Books, 1989.

Ornish, Dean. *Reversing Heart Disease.* New York: Random House, 1990.

Ornstein, Robert and Sobel, David. *The Healing Brain.* New York: Simon and Schuster, 1987.

Pelletier, Kenneth R. *Mind as Healer, Mind as Slayer.* New York: Delta, 1977.

Peterson, Christopher. *Health and Optimism.* New York: MacMillan, 1991.

Pickering, George. *Creative Malady.* New York: Dell, 1974.

Pitzele, Sefra Kobrin. *We Are Not Alone.* New York: Workman Publishing, 1986.

Reading, Chris M., and Meillon, Ross S. *Your Family Tree Connection.* New Canaan, CT: Keats Publishing, 1988.

Roger, John and McWilliams, Peter. *You Can't Afford the Luxury of a Negative Thought.* Los Angeles: Prelude Press, 1988.

Sacks, Oliver. *A Leg to Stand On.* New York: Perennial Library, 1984.

Seligman, Martin E. P. *Helplessness.* San Francisco: W. H. Freeman & Co., 1975.

Seligman, Martin E. P. *Learned Optimism.* New York: Alfred A. Knopf, 1991.

Shealy, C. Norman, and Myers, Caroline M. *The Creation of Health.* Walpole, NH: Stillpoint, 1988.

Shellenberger, Sylvia, Shurden, Kay W. and Treadwell, T. Walter, Jr. Faculty training seminars in family systems. *Family Medicine,* Vol. 20, No. 3, May-June 1988.

Shute, Nancy. How healthy is your family tree? *Hippocrates,* Vol. 2 88–89, Jan-Feb. 1988.

Siegel, Bernie. *Love, Medicine & Miracles.* New York: Harper & Row, 1986.

Simonton, O. Carl, Matthews-Simonton, Stephanie H. and Creighton, James. *Getting Well Again.* Los Angeles: J. P. Tarcher, 1978.

Spiegel, Penina. *McQueen: The Untold Story of a Bad Boy.* New York: Doubleday, 1986.

Spiro, Howard M. *Doctors, Patients and Placebos.* New Haven: Yale University Press.

Tate, David A. *Health, Hope and Healing.* New York: M. Evans & Co., 1989.

Thomas, Lewis. *The Medusa and the Snail.* New York: Viking Press, 1979.

Todd, Alexander T. *Intimate Adversaries: Cultural Conflict Between Doctors and Women Patients.* Phila.: University of Pennsylvania Press, 1989.

West, Candace. *Between Doctors and Patients.* Indiana University Press, 1984.

West, Red, West, Sonny and Hebler, Dave. Elvis, *What Happened?* New York: Ballantine Books, 1977.

Zborowski, Mark. *People in Pain,* San Francisco: Jossey-Bass, 1969.

Index

Joan C. Barth, Ph.D., has conducted a family therapy practice in Doylestown, Pennsylvania for the past twenty years. She is Co-Director of The Therapists' Center, which provides psychotherapists with additional training. Dr. Barth, Secretary of the International Family Therapy Association, is a featured speaker and provider of seminars both nationally and internationally. Married, mother of two and grandmother of one, Dr. Barth knows the family life cycle not only from study but from personal experience.